Confessions Of a
Drunken Sailor

Confessions Of a Drunken Sailor

Charles Torres

To order additional copies of this book, contact:
Xlibris
844-714-8691
www.Xlibris.com
Orders@Xlibris.com
822257

Tbale of Contents

DEDICATION

This book is dedicated to those shipmates that
I served with in the United States Navy from
September of 1984 thru April of 1990.
Those with whom I served onboard the USS
Proteus, Nuclear Submarine Support Ship stationed
in the homeport of Guam from 1985 thru 1988.
This book is a story of the extraordinary
experiences of young sailors stationed overseas
in exotic ports through Western Pacific
cruises, ports-o-call that gave us unforgettable
memories and enduring friendship

Chapter 1

PERMISSION GRANTED
TO COME ABOARD

A house fly twitches my forehead waking me, head is throbbing. Dry pasty tongue and crusty lips, eyes slowly open, surroundings unfamiliar. Look around through the glint of bloodshot pupils, tiny specs of dust rise into thin sunbeams that pierce the open holes through the walls of a grass hut. Entwined in long, silky, spider web of black hair, a bar girl still sleeps. Empty bamboo cup with the words ``Gorilla Juice " painted in bright fluorescent colors lies amongst a pile of clothing tossed in the corner. The buzz of little motorcycle engines in the distance, rooster crowing, begins a new day in Barrio Barretto, Philippines. Shaking away the morning hangover, I realize got to get back. Where the hell am I? What is this place? Rising from a hard feather matted mattress, attempting not to wake the girl. Quietly crawling to the corner, checking my watch amongst the clothes…7 o'clock…I've got to hurry up, can't be late, last day. My mind wanders. Slowly I gather up the cigarette smoke saturated clothes and pull them on. Stuffing a 100 peso bill into the bamboo cup, push open the creaky little door of the hut. One last glance behind at that exotic little beauty still sleeping soundly, I emerge from the opening. Sun light blinds me. Stumbling down a steep muddy road dotted with stone puddles, enter the village and seek a jeep née bus back to Subic. Scratching at the ground, chickens wander and cluck. Finding the bottom of the muddy road, heat waves glimmer. In the distance, my sun-baked eyes see a Jeep nee arriving. Struggling to keep my balance the heat and humidity begins to play with my equilibrium. Stepping out slightly waving my hands in the air as the jeep nee comes to a stop. Pulling up into the back of the multi-colored vehicle the driver hollers back in broken English, "10 peso to the main gate". Digging deep into nearly empty pockets, the clinking coins, Do I have enough here? With a half burnt brain, swishing the coins within my hand I add the correct change, "Whew" didn't know if I had anything left. Fumbling the money up to the driver, slumping down into the torn seat covers of the jeep nee' benches, and trying to stabilize my swirling head. The only American on the bus disheveled and hung-over the villagers started. The driver hits the gas pedal and the jeep nee pulls forward. Heavy belches of diesel fumes fill the cabin. The bumpy ride sloshing my stomach, the sun baking my face, my head near to explosion, the smell of diesel fuel, puking was not an option. Anticipating my arrival at the main gate to the base, I contemplate the end to this miserable hangover. A cup of over brewed extra black tank juice and a few aspirin usually do the trick. Easing back into my seat amongst the villagers, I turn my head from their gaze as my fingers massage my now sweating forehead. My mind reverses back to the decision to bring me to this place, how did I get here? What the hell am I doing in this place? Take me back... back to the beginning. My name is Charlie Torres, and I'm a sailor in the United States Navy.

SMALL COW FARM IN LOWER ALABAMA – FALL 1983

Slocomb Alabama, a small farming community settled just over the Alabama border of the panhandle of Florida was my mother's idea of keeping me out of trouble from the spring break beaches of Panama City Florida. That's where I grew up. Having moved here in the previous year from Panama City, I was a fish out of water to say the least. Beach kid in a farming community where families have been rooted since the Civil War. It's the weekend before my senior year in high school, and heaving bales of hay to a rusty T-Rex toothed conveyor belt from the back of a flat-bed truck, hay particles bellow up into my face and dangle from the long locks of heavy metal hair. Coughing, raise my head to wipe the sweat and dust from my dirty face. Taking the bottom of my faded concert t-shirt soaked with sweat, it does the job quite nicely. Pausing from the conveyor, unscrewing my canteen and taking a slug. You see, I had decided to help my girlfriend Melanie's father Carl bale hay for a few bucks for new school clothes. Having no real source of income and being poor, my options were limited on opportunity. Carl, an old fashioned country boy that knew everything about farming and carpentry, was the typical southern man's man. Coveralls and dirty boots, he enjoyed the laborious tasks that his little farm had to offer. I began to wonder if it was worth it. Carl doing his duty to instill his traditional hard working values into this beach kid, "You've got to get down amongst it! You're falling behind, keep up with the conveyor belt!" he yelled. I prayed for a reprieve from this inhuman task. Bale after bale, rising with every clink and clank of the baling conveyer, plopping over the end. Lifting and stacking, and doing it all over again one field after the other until the barn was stacked full. The hay had to last all winter. Carl was taking too much pleasure showing this beach kid with the rock-n-roll hair, how things were done down here on the farm. As if an answer to my prayers of reprieve, my girlfriend Melanie, with her southern accent calls from the house, "Y'all want some sweet tea? We have something made come on in and take a break". Carl grumbles, "I guess that we need a break", and reluctantly pushes the red stop button on the conveyor. It screeches and grinds to a halt leaving un-stacked bales of hay remaining on the ground. Removing the hot leather gloves from my sweaty hands, I hop down off the truck. I had worked up an appetite and was looking forward to what Melanie and her Mother had in store. We head to the house and wash up. Leftover buttered cornbread and beans. Little soup bowls aligned so perfectly with folded napkins and silverware are placed upon the table. Bean stew and cornbread should take the edge off our hunger. After washing up Carl seats himself in front of his usual spot at the table and says grace. We all bow our heads as Melanie flirts with me by peeking under her lashes during his prayer. Amen, we all say together and place our napkins neatly upon our laps. Plowing his spoon deep into his bowl of beans Carl stuffs each spoonful as if it were his last. Garbling through a half full gob he asks, "So what are you going to do after high school Charles?" Caught off guard I think to myself, seventeen years old with no real expectations of college, I really hadn't given much thought to my future. I mean really, no money equals no options. I knew I didn't like baling hay. But Carl was curious as to what I had in store for myself and for possibly his daughter. I wanted a clean job, something with a future. But what answer was I going to give Carl, the father of my girlfriend. His old fashioned expectations of young men in the south still prevail. Getting down on one knee and propose as soon as adulthood comes around. "Computers or Business", I replied to Carl. Trying to sound as if I had a game plan. Of course he was concerned about his daughter dating a loser. "Computers are the place to be. They say that's the future" Carl said. "Have you seen that new arcade game, what's it called, Space Invaders…man the technology. Yes if I was young that's what I would do." Space Invaders had been out for some time, but that's how far backwards Carl still was. I thought, computers, well maybe but how. We finished our bowls of bean soup and tea. "Well let's get back to work. It's not gettin' done by itself" Carl said, and it was back to the old flatbed truck to bale more hay.

Dusk fell and stacking the last bale of hay in the barn I was ready for the day to end. I'm exhausted. Carl pushes the red stop button on the conveyor one last time and again the spine tingling screech of the rusty contraption grinds to a halt. Carl," Well that should do it, thank you for the help today Charles" Anticipating my reward like a dog outside a butcher shop I wait patiently for Carl to pay me. He reaches into his hole ridden overalls and pulls a sweaty leather billfold from the torn back pocket. Taking a couple of sweat soaked twenties from the wallet, "An honest day's work, for an honest day's pay" I certainly have earned every sweaty penny. Thankful for the opportunity, I'm anxious to get home and wash the layers of hay soot and sweat from my tired carcass. "So long Melanie, I'll call you tomorrow", as I plop into the front seat of my mother's car.

Lying in bed that night, my long heavy metal hair wet and perfumed from the Strawberry Suave shampoo, the radio tuned to the only hard rock station in lower Alabama, I adjusted the volume. Turning the pages to the JC Penny sales circulars to shop for last minute deals on school clothes, Red ball point pen in hand, I circle the pictures of the items that catch my fancy. Shoes, shirts and maybe a pair of blue jeans, I think that will do it. Bam! Bam! Bam! The pleasant ambiance is broken. Banging outside my bedroom door, "Turn that devil music down!" screeches my mother. O.k.! Turning down the radio, continuing to sing the words to Van Halen's Mean Street. My mind wanders as I dread the new school year which is only one day away. A beach kid amongst the farm boys of the largest peanut growing community in Alabama, and really didn't connect with the culture, a far cry from the sugar white sands of the Florida panhandle. A misfit for I am certain the farm boys will buy up the latest style of cowboy boots, and I choose a pair of cheap sneakers from the catalog circular, "These look pretty cool", circling the shoes with the red pen I've been chewing on, I turn and click off the light and settle down for the night.

As the weekend ticked away and my family and I made a trip into the only mall in lower southeast Alabama to get those shoes, the first day of school arrives early the next morning. Monday morning arrives. I wait outside my house for the bus stop with my new shoes and old jeans. Turns out I didn't have enough money to buy all the new clothes I had circled. So I took the shoes. The yellow school bus squeaks to a stop in front of our house. I and my siblings, brother and sisters board the bus. Curious faces of the crowded bus stare at us as we enter. We walk down the aisle amongst the freckled faces of farming kids staring at us. Pondering where to sit, my sisters, find a seat easily. Searching for a seat down the aisle I wonder who will allow my brother and me to sit next to them. Luckily one of the privileged, allows us to be seated next to him. Careful not to scuff my new shoes, my brother and I pack into the seat. The ride is tight and awkward, as the old bus bumps along the narrow country roads.

Slocomb high school, a small farm town school with about 400 students, is around the next turn and the parking lot is filled with school buses, car loads of kids and the pick-up trucks of the seniors. Our bus slowly pulls into the parking lot. Staring out from the sliding windows of the bus, a typical mix of student groups is already forming, jocks, honor roll kids, the smokers and tobacco dippers, the cowboys and the cheerleaders, each getting acclimated to each other and to the surroundings. Each group of kids that have virtually grown up together seems to know each other without missing a beat. No new school for them it seems. Stepping off the bus and onto the sidewalk, thankfully my last year of school, I stayed the loner. Alone and quiet taking it all in, waiting for the bell. Finding a place near the doors anticipating an end to the isolation of being the new kid.

The school bell rings and the students flood the doors and scramble through the hallways, new schedule in their hands, finding their classes. Brand new sneakers squeak on freshly waxed floors echo through the hallways as hundreds of students scatter in every direction. "Hey Mrs. Smith," as the students file past classrooms with already familiar teachers. Bumping my way through the noisy halls, I find my home room and take a seat. This one seems pretty good as I settle into the old wood and steel desk. Sitting in my home room as my senior year in high school began, it was the same old thing that I had observed before. The popular kids kicked off the year with bright smiles and bright futures, greeted each other and took freshly cleaned desks next to each other. Seemingly relishing their little bubble of reality. Silly laughing and crazy behavior, an obvious attempt at getting undo attention to once again become popular. I apparently was sitting to close within their realm. As if to shoo a pesky fly, "Um, do you think you could move over there?" one of the cheerleaders asks me. Bubbling over with her brace face smile she seemed unaffected by her request. Because of just the sheer unadulterated positive, smiley way in which she asked I complied. "Sure, no problem" I replied. Gathering my things I politely oblige and move to a desk far away from their domain. Not even a thank you was to follow, as her other friends settled into their comfy little world amongst each other. Giggling and smacking their bubble gum as if their encounter with me was of utter inconsequence.

Being shunned by the other students I had accepted the current state of affairs. Struggling to find my identity, I thought about happier times. This past summer I met my father after several years of divorce.

During the summer I had gone to visit my father in Los Angeles. I wondered how life could have been different if my parents had stayed together. I wondered, would I be able to go to college if that were the case. Would I be visiting college campuses and discussing with my friends my future after high school. I contemplated living with my father and getting out of this country boy setting, the southern accent and antebellum demeanor really not my thing. So my choices were L.A. or lower Alabama, some would say L.A. stands for lower Alabama as well, but the differences in culture are quite opposite. I found myself enduring the high school experience within the confines of Slocomb High School...for now.

Plodding through the school year, and squeaking by on my grades, I wondered what the future held. Would I be successful, where would I start? Would I achieve the American Dream? No money for college? The other kids in school were talking about what college they were going to attend and so on. With no real guidance from a working single mom and dad not in the picture, I put the idea out of my head.

Midway through the school year and sloughing through the halls one day the Navy recruiter, Petty Officer 1st class Newhart, happened to be at the school. Standing in the halls between classes in his snazzy dress white uniform I was intrigued. Walking past the Navy man he nodded his head politely and continued his conversation with one of the prettier teachers. "So I can reach you at this number?" I heard him say to Ms. Tanner, a buxom brunette whom all the guys thought was sexy. You know every high school has one sexy teacher. She chuckles with a flirty smile," I must get to my class" folding a tiny piece of paper that she shuffles into his hand. I thought "hey that uniform really does the trick". He smiles and stuffs the paper into his pocket as if it were routine. The idea of the military had never occurred to me. But that uniform and its effects really got me thinking about it.

Newhart paid a few more visits to the school during the next few months and each time I got the nod of hello how ya doin'. Until one day, Newhart decides to extend a handshake and say "What's your name kid?"

By now my new sneakers had become worn and mucky. And new clothes to me were hand me downs that my older brother found out of his closet and granted them to me out of pity. My haggard clothing was certainly a clue that the Navy could be a better opportunity for me, recruiter Newhart saw easy prey. He told me of the opportunities the Navy provided, three hot meals a day, free medical care, free housing, money for college, even learn a trade. And of course see the world! "Well I don't know" I said cautiously. "Why don't you come to my office and watch a video, you know just to figure it out?" Newhart baited me. I thought about what else I have to do, so that afternoon went to the recruiter's office and watched the video. The video explained what the Navy was about and showed sailors on liberty in foreign ports, laughing and having fun.

It didn't take much to convince me that this was the only opportunity that I had besides baling hay and inevitably, Newhart found his way back to my house that evening. My mother realized that this was probably the best opportunity available to me, and agreed to sign the papers for this 17 year old recruit over our modest supper, gravy and two day old biscuits. She signed away while the recruiter sopped his biscuit into the bottom of a cast iron pan. Getting those last few nuggets of tender meat tidbits mixed within that thick country gravy. Newhart pointed to all of the blank lines for the signatures, "Right here Ms. Torres" his gob half full. She signed each and every blank space and I contemplated this could be the first step in my future and would it be a good investment into myself and the country. I was struggling to find the value. Would it be a way out from poverty and could I find myself in the process.

As the year rolled on and I realized I was miserable in lower Alabama, not really fitting in, my mother finally gave in and allowed me to move to Los Angeles to live with my father. I couldn't wait to get packed but regretted leaving my girlfriend behind for a long distance relationship. Merely children who thought we were in love. Plus I thought a little time away wouldn't hurt. So grabbing a cheap flight on Continental airlines, I flew back out to Los Angeles to the big grin and open arms of my father. He was anxious and happy to experience one of his kids going to school under his guidance. I finished my senior year of high school in Los Angeles, a big adjustment from lower Alabama. Keeping my long distance relationship with Melanie, I learned that life in the big city can be intimidating, scary and dangerous. But being a naïve high school kid who didn't know any better I made the best of the situation and made many good friends and enjoyed the experience that only Los Angeles can provide.

Climbing down the rocks at Huntington Beach to go surfing, camping trips to Big Bear Lake, hiking the trails at Chantry Flats were fun and eventful. Hiding from police helicopter search lights that swoops the beaches late at night and rock concerts at the L.A.

Amphitheatre and of course the little weekend trips to Knotts Berry Farm and Six Flags, were a blast and a welcome distraction from my circumstances from which I came. My father wanted to make up lost time and fatherly memories by spoiling me rotten. He regretted the loss of those times and wanted me to experience some form of happiness. But there was one place that really made an impression on me, the Griffith Park Observatory. My friends and I met there for the Pink Floyd Laser light show. We all piled into our friends' car and hung out in the parking lot horsing around and listening to music. While waiting for the show to begin, I ventured away from my group for a second to take in the view. It was on the overlook patio that I discovered the view of Los Angeles all lit up and sparkling. It dawned on me what a vast difference in culture and lifestyle that I had made coming to California. I reflected on my life and wondered how the cities of the world would stack up against this magnificent skyline once I was in the Navy.

There on the hillside with my friends, I felt normal, I fit in. For once I had been accepted by friends that liked me for me, and expected nothing. No popularity contest, just being me. I appreciated the change that I had made, but all good things must come to an end and graduation was upon the Alhambra High School class of 1984 and I knew that this all would soon be over.

The day had come to walk the stage in cap and gown. Thousands of students and parents packed the campus at Cal State L.A. for our commencement. The cheers from proud parents filled the campus as the graduates filed up the stairs and one by one accepted their diplomas. My father beaming from ear to ear was able to see one of his kids graduate. I couldn't believe that I had made it through high school and the evening of graduation was one to remember. My family and friends all congratulated each other with a glass of champagne, the cork pops, as we cut into the cake and passed around my diploma for all to see. Then, my dad gave me my graduation gift. Everyone stood around as I opened the shiny gift wrapping. Peeling away the edges and opening the box, it was a camera for those foreign countries that I was about to visit. I was going to miss these people and the good memories of those that have accepted me.

The smiles would soon fade and the applause quiet as it was time to become a sailor. A sobering thought that I must return to Alabama for processing into the United States Navy. I resigned myself to the choice, the only choice, that I had made and accepted my fate.

One last trip up the hill to Griffith Park, to take a last look at the city that welcomed me when I was alone. This little hill that overlooks the Los Angeles skyline had become a place of reflection for me, a place where I could think and contemplate life, it had become sentimental to me. Seeing the massive skyline with its twinkling lights and bustling traffic gave me pause to think of all those beneath their struggle against the necessities of life, that it wasn't just my burden. I wondered how I could attain such wealth and success. I pondered, was the military a good stepping stone? Was it a good starting point, it gave me hope.

It was a long goodbye to my friends and family in Los Angeles and it was back to Alabama. My youth and high school days were over and I reflected on those students with the bright smiles and bright futures and wondered if their parents had them packed for their life in college. If they thought of every detail, the credit cards, the bank accounts with plenty of spending money, the new books and the dorm room. I thought of their tears when dad and mom got that last hug from little Johnnie or Stacey and they drove back home in their new cars, leaving them for their experience in college. I contemplated how different my life was and looked forward to the opportunity ahead of me. What would my experience be?

Back in Alabama, a rainy morning arrives and it's time to report to the recruiting office. My home is quiet and resolute as my sisters help me pack my bag. Tears in their eyes they know our childhood experiences have come to an end as I was now leaving those behind and embarking upon my adult life. Teary hugs and a quiet ride to the recruiting station in my mother's little car as the raindrops plopped on the windshield. Wipers squeak back and forth, back and forth. My mothers' tears are rolling down her cheeks, hugging my neck. She knows I'm not coming back. I'm beginning my life without her. She cries "I'm sorry son I wish I could do more". The little car comes to a stop at the recruiting station. "I know mom... I'll be fine" trying to comfort her she hugs my neck goodbye. Slamming the car door as I exit with my bag, Petty Officer Newhart loads up a van full of his new recruits. "Come on Torres you're late". I cram my bag into the back and push into the last space in the seats. Waving to my mom, Newhart starts the engine and begins to drive us to the Greyhound bus depot. Swiping her windshield to clear the condensation from her view, my mother's teary face fades into the distance. Slocomb was now a distant memory.

Arriving at the bus station we all heaved our bags onto the parking lot and entered the bus station. Taking our seats lined along the large dust coated windows the smoke filled bus lobby is full of travelers. Men with haggard clothes and grey whiskers yawn while reading their crumpled newspapers, Young children running about without concern for the wet muddy floor, and transients just looking to ride until they discover a new city in which to find a free meal. And of course brand new Navy recruits on our way to boot camp. With our tickets in hand we each take our turn at the clunky vending machine in the corner to buy cigarettes and stale chocolate bars. When finally our bus number is called over the intercom, we gather up our bags. "Well I guess this is it you guys" Newhart says. We all board the bus and take a seat. The smell of stale cigarette smoke and the blue water toilet fill the interior of the bus cabin. Looking out the window we all see Petty Officer Newhart, with that snazzy uniform, is standing at attention and saluting, Yelling up to the windows he bids farewell in typical seafarer fashion, "Fair Winds and Following Seas!" he yells up to his recruits. The typical sailor salutation he snaps his salute to his side turns into the bus terminal and disappears into anonymousness. He had done his duty.

1984 MEDICAL EXAMINATION AND PROCESSING STATION (M.E.P.S.) – MONTGOMERY, ALABAMA

Reveille, Reveille, early morning wake-up call several groggy-eyed, bed-head and bad breathed Moe-mo, walking around in dirty skivvies yawn and pushing into the bathroom to brush up. The rude awakening at the MEPS (Medical Examination and Processing Station) isn't exactly the Hilton. This was the first stage of organized confusion just before being sent into the pits of hell, San Diego Recruit Training Command for the United States Navy. The night before the condemned souls telling stories of why they made the choice to join the most famous canoe club in the world was the pitiful commentary. Lying in the metal framed beds with the blue striped feather mattresses, my roommates describe their reasons for joining. Some had different reasons, tired of being at home with the parents, nothing else better going on, some of the older men their last chance for anything etc. For me it was poverty, the military being a venue to escape my childhood circumstances. This decision weighed on my mind as my current state of circumstances had given me this rude awakening. It was time to get to the chow hall and get breakfast. Standing in the chow line at the MEPS station "Load it up with the eggs and baby poop", the man next to me retorts. The cook obliges the request with a swift plop of the runny grits onto his tray. I learn the military lingo quickly. "Baby poop as well", as my turn in the chow line comes up. Baby poop, green tinted eggs, and cold margarine buttered toast, and some heavy black tank juice. Scanning the chow hall for a place to sit amongst the diverse mixture of people, all with different backgrounds, it was difficult to find a place to fit in. As if back on the school bus, I settled into a place with my recruit buddies. "Over here Torres", one of them shouts. We settle in and eat our first taste of government issued eggs and grits. Wondering what was in store. After finishing our breakfasts a petty officer barking orders began to bellow at the exit, a schedule of tests quizzes and turning your head and cough was the regimen of the day. We all were directed by sharp dressed and uniformed Navy Petty Officers from one station to the next. Roll call after breakfast we line up in the main hall, the petty officer, "Abraham!" "Here" replies Abraham. "Benton!" the petty officer yells. No answer then a pause. "Benton! Answer up, is Benton here?", "Here" Benton replies. The petty officer calls out the list; he calls my name, "Torres!" I reply with a quick "Here". "O.k. Listen up. Today you will undergo several exams and if you obey orders it will go smoothly" the petty officer instructed us to the different rooms for written exams and filling out forms.

The yawns in the old classrooms continue to the late hours of the morning until the medical exams in the afternoon. All of the new soon to be recruits were led to another wing of the MEPS building for the physicals. Medical Corpsmen dressed in white smocks in each little examination room, "O.k. open and stick out your tongue".

I open my mouth for the examination. The corpsman takes my blood pressure, weight and height. Pretty routine stuff until we came into the dreaded prostate gland examination room. A prostate exam is standard procedure for all wishing to move on to the next phase of our processing. No way around the little room with the two mysterious doors. Within the main examination room two benches were alongside each other, cold white tile floors and metal mini blinds that covered the old window panes, two smaller examination rooms with long body tables. The corpsman enters and orders us to pull a number from the dispenser and disrobe our underwear and stand along the benches until our number is called. There were two medical personnel there, one an older woman with a gentle smile and neatly pinned red hair. Not too intimidating depending on what was about to occur to all of us, she seemed comforting as she came into and out of the examination room after each patient, with her white jacket and squeaky shoes. The other examiner was the picture of an obese German born giant with Wiener schnitzel for fingers. The gasp that entered the room when he emerged from the examination room filled our minds with the worst prospect ever. The word "next" was never meant to be so dreaded. But as the medical examiners entered and emerged from the examination rooms we all pondered our fate as to how our individual luck would pan out. Would I get the gentle red haired nurse or the Giant German with the schnitzel for fingers? With each number called we all looked at our tickets as if it were the lottery from prostate exam hell. And as luck would have it luck was on my side this day. Some of the others weren't so lucky.

Having been sworn in the day was drawing to a close and we were given a set of orders. Stay for another night until our flight to our recruit training, boot camp. My orders were for the next day. That night I pondered the life I left and my girl back home as I stared at her picture, the only token of that life that brought me brief happiness. Ironically I wanted to leave my old life behind. I was anxious to start into the unknown of military life. The next morning we all ate that government issue breakfast again and were loaded onto an old grey bus with no air conditioning and cracked leather seating. And although my experience so far was the typical government no frills ride, I hadn't realized yet that I was on my way to the greatest adventure of my life. My orders were to the recruit training command in San Diego California for eight weeks of Naval Basic training.

During the flight to California I was onboard the plane with some others that were in for the same experience as I, San Diego Recruit Training Command. This group of soon to be sailors discussed the rumors of the total experience of boot camp. Rumors from long lost uncles and cousins that have gone to boot camp before filled the conversation within the airplane. The stories of the hardships of boot camp and the drill instructors that showed no mercy filled our minds with trepidation. However, nothing would prepare us for the real experience. We settled into the flight across the country and enjoyed the last comforts of deserts and other airplane food before we delved into the horrors of the dreaded boot camp. After four hours in the air we finally landed.

Soon after landing at San Diego international airport, we left the plane and headed to baggage claim. After gathering our luggage we waited for our ride to the next destination, the recruit depot. It was dusk outside and standing around smoking and joking outside the automatic doors of the airport, we felt sorry for the pitiful Marine Corp recruits that had been standing at attention since they arrived already being barked at by a Marine Drill Instructor. Eventually another government-issue grey bus as ugly as the first soon came to a squalling halt in front of our group. Soon our little worlds would come crashing down the same as those poor marine recruits who were already having their personal experience with boot camp.

The doors to the old grey bus swung open. A Brutus beefcake petty officer with tack ironed dungarees and perfectly curled Dixie cup hat barks, "Hurry up and get in". His gruff growl and rolled sleeves expose a half inked tattoo slightly emerging below the cuff line. Again we boarded this bus with our hard trimmed sailor driver, this time the last bus for two months until recruit training was over. The sun had faded and only the tips of glowing cigarettes illuminated the darkness in the bus as we rode to the training depot. The driver shifts the gears. With each pull from the driver's hard grip on the gear shift the gears grind and clank on the old bus. Curious, anticipation filled our minds as we stopped at a sentry gate at the entrance to the base. Light conversation amongst all the new recruits continue to speculate on what the next unknown experience may be. The bus begins to slow as it arrives at the gate. A uniformed gate sentry salutes the bus as he opens the gate waiving us through. The bus enters the training command and winds down a narrow dirt road.

A receiving building with pale yellow lights begins to appear. As the bus stops at the receiving building, outside, a group of khaki uniformed men stand at the edge of a parking lot with yellow feet shapes painted in neat rows upon its surface. The quiet driver stood up and turned around and immediately transformed into a barking drill instructor shouting, "Shut up! And get your asses out on the grinder!" An immediate quiet panic consumed us as we hurried to get our things and out onto the pavement. The shapes of feet were painted onto the pavement and were spaced neatly apart as a group of Company Commanders were barking orders and getting us in line. "Get out of that Goddamn bus you little Shits! Quickly" Our nightmare had become reality as our pity for the Marine recruits became our own reality. "Get your feet on those spots and line up!"

Several dog-faced Chief Petty officers with khaki uniforms bark and place the new recruits in orderly rows. One recruit, distracted by our bus driver emerging from the bus and standing with a sharp parade rest in front, "What are you lookin' at Shit-ball!" shouts a Company Commander. "Don't even look at him!" pointing at the driver, "You haven't earned the right to look at him Recruit eyes front!" We were all introduced to our new father for eight weeks, Company Commander Peterson. Peterson, a gruff, rough and tumble, Harley Davidson kind of guy introduces himself as our new Dad. "Mommy and Daddy aren't here now you little fucks I'm your new daddy!" Taking issue with a long haired, beer bellied kid with a Harley Davidson shirt," Do you have a Harley recruit?" Peterson barks. "No sir", replied the kid. "Oh, so you're just tryin' to look tough! Recruit, Welcome to hell!" I wondered if this hell would be worth all of my future agony, the sacrifice of the rigors of military life, have I made the right choice. I began to question the soundness of my path to success. We begin our military adventure by entering the unknown, into the receiving building.

After being segregated into separate companies, the buzz haircut and a series of inoculation shots, we went to outfitting our uniforms and soon forgot about civilian life. Our new destiny was in full swing and I must admit that seeing my rock and roll long hair hit the barbershop floor was an adjustment. Continually rubbing the stubble of my now shaved head, I couldn't get over the shock of being bald. Dog tired from the long flight and had no sleep until taps, we were in for a long day. A rigid regimen of formation, P.T. (Physical Training), meals, classes, military training, drills, chemical weapons, fire control training and inspections was the course of action until graduation, organized misery. This is where I met Seaman Recruit Tiffalo. A Midwestern Missouri kid with a slow smart-ass demeanor became my bunkmate. Since the bunk arrangement was in alphabetical order, Tiffalo and I began all of our daily tasks together. Making our bunks, inspections, clean up and uniform maintenance, we shine our boon-dockers. We learn to line up in formation and march until our shin splints and feet ache. We learn the basic skills of recruit training that all sailors go through in boot camp. Several days of regimented class room indoctrination and tasks that we will learn as a crewman aboard one of Ronald Reagan's big six hundred ship navy.

As a few days pass it's our turn in the Olympic size swimming pool for survival at sea training, "So Charlie, did you expect all this?" he asks as we wait for our turn to jump off a 25 foot platform for abandon ship drills, "Yeah" I reply. "Are you ready for this one?" he asks. "I'm ready for anything." He has realized that this is no cake walk. Boot camp has proven to test us all, our mental and physical strength. Our ability to understand and problem solve, and most of all our perseverance. Jumping into the cold water those who could swim would survive the deep water drill and those who couldn't would be weeded out and trained to swim. The Navy Seals conducting the drill were not very forgiving as some of the recruits who couldn't swim were barked at mercilessly, and fished out of the pool with long poles. Our turn arrived. Standing atop the platform I looked down at the swimming pool and the shimmering water. I contemplated the drop as I crossed my arms and ankles as was the proper form for abandon ship drills. The whistle blew and off the platform I plunged. The fall felt endless as I finally entered the deep end of the Olympic sized swimming pool. I felt fortunate that those trips to the beach in my childhood prepared me for this moment. The Seals observed us all as they observed if we could tread water and swim one hundred yards after a few laps around the pool. The whistle finally blew that the drill was over. Out of the pool and shivering on the benches, Tiffalo and I watched as the remaining recruits took their turn at the drill.

The next drills were fire fighting and gas attack training. Fire fighting in a dark space onboard a burning naval vessel was an integral part of training. Walking through dark passageways on a real naval ship that had been attacked and on fire was a real possibility without the benefit of breathing gear. This was the scenario prior to entering a controlled space for fighting a test fire. We were taught to fight the fire with teamwork and determination, as the ship was our only refuge out in the open ocean. Without the ship, we all would be in the water and the chances for survival were slim if that should ever occur. Two and four inch fire hoses with teams of four put out space fires and oil fires. Different types of fires were identified and the proper fire fighting techniques were drilled within us. Foam or water only, or using breathing apparatus were the tools and equipment that were taught to us. We were becoming trained sailors without fear.

"You will now learn to control your fear of gas attack" barked company commander Peterson. He marched his recruits in front of a plain concrete block building with just a few steps leading to a metal door. One entrance and exit on each end of the building. After a brief training session on the use of a gas mask we entered the building. Once inside we lined up in formation. Peterson and other company commanders were seated within an enclosure behind a large plexiglass window. Peterson leaned forward and spoke into a microphone, "Can you hear me?"... "Sir yes Sir!" shouted the recruits. "You will recite general order number two on my command". Ordered to remove our masks we all comply. Immediately the sting of tear gas fills our eyes, noses and lungs. "What is general order number two?!" Peterson shouted into the microphone. Huffing and coughing together trying to recite general order number two, we struggled "To walk my post in a military manner, keeping always on the alert, observing everything with sight or hearing Sir!" All within the chamber perform this drill together or it is done over and over again. Once finished, emerge from the chamber coughing and choking away the gas from our sinuses and lungs, vomiting from the exposure. Essential training if ever attacked biologically or chemically.

Physical training is a daily regimen of high impact exercise. Long marches and running was the daily prescription along with calisthenics. Chief Peterson competes with the Marine recruits jogging in unison at the Marine Recruit Training command next door across the chain link fence. "Keep your steps and don't let those grunts show you all up!" he commanded. Huffing and puffing I wondered if those were the same marine recruits that I remembered at the airport.

Clean and folded uniforms, tightly made bunks, inspection quality barracks that were kept needed and tidy at all times. Shit, shower and shave in twenty minutes then muster on the barracks floor for inspection, close shave and trimmed fingernails, clean skivvies rounded out a series of daily inspections.

Our experience in boot camp was checkered with disciplinary exercise mashing episodes after lights out, this as a result mostly of bonehead mistakes. Company Commander Peterson took out his aggression on us all under the guise of turning his recruits into trained sailors ready for war. Up at 4:30 a.m. and in bed by 9:00 p.m. the days were long and tiresome.

It was Tiffalo's and my turn to clean the head one evening after chow. Breaking the silent swipes of heavy thick stringed swabs, Tiffalo exclaims, "This fucking sucks. If I'd known this I wouldn't have joined". "So then what would have you done?" I asked. He pondered for a moment and went back to quietly mopping. I sympathized with his misery as mine was the same. I didn't want to consider this misery as being a mistake, but rather a stepping stone to something better. Besides, it was my only choice in the grand scheme of making a future for myself, or was that just a dream. Was it a dream that was unreachable reserved only for the privileged in our society? I didn't want to believe it. But thinking back to those college kids in the dorm, my experience was becoming quite different.

Given collateral duties each recruit applied special skills that were acquired prior to boot camp. Mine was company yeoman. I took care of all the individual paperwork for the recruits within the company. Keeping track of inoculation records, discipline records and other files, I spent many hours in Peterson's office. During those hours, seemingly hidden by Peterson, tucked in amongst training notebooks and military journals, I noticed Peterson had a photo album of his motorcycle trips. Curious I pulled it from amongst the others. Flipping the pages of photos of a 1980 Harley bagger, Peterson had managed to document some of his road trips. While turning mid-way through the album I discovered he had photos of his girlfriend, a hot little Harley chick naked and frolicking in various poses upon his bike. "Holy Shit!" I thought to myself. Being deprived of female company and naked photos considered contraband, I seized the opportunity for a little taste of the soft world outside the gates. Of course I couldn't keep my little secret from my shipmates. For candy, cigarettes and other favors, I managed to create a little cottage industry for a little peek at Petersons' album. Also, a little payback to Chief Peterson for all the mashing episodes as well, revenge well deserved. "Hey Tif, take a look at this"...Tiffalo takes a long hard look... "Dude if Peterson catches you with this..."...I didn't care. "Uh, Tif, that will be one cigarette"...collecting my fee.

Of course the company had a sweet hearts board with all the pictures of our girlfriends for all to enjoy. Pictures of wives and girlfriends from all parts of the country were neatly pinned upon a cork board that was hung near the Company Commanders office. Country girls from the Midwest corn belt, and sexy wives from Texas and Louisiana. California blondes and New York brunettes, they were all beautiful. I gladly pinned my girl's picture to the board, a blue eyed brunette from a small town in Alabama. Just before the end of boot camp we all voted on the best sweetheart. A lovely Hawaiian island honey with a bright smile, dark tan and those lovely hips in a tiny floral bikini won the company sweetheart award.

Upon graduation, the day we all marched to leave this little corner of hell, Company Commander Peterson congratulated us all who had made it. Company 939 had won every award. Captain's trophy, and all the banners and flags that make a particular company the cream of the crop.

Tiffalo and I were going on to our schools together. Peterson paused before we all packed our sea bags for transfer to the school barracks. Collecting his things from his office and packing them in a box he paused briefly when putting away his photo album and asked, "So I'm just curious, how many of you have seen my photo album?"...Amongst 80 men in those barracks packing their sea bags and rolling up blankets, they paused, looked over at each other fearing repercussion, slowly, reluctantly, cautiously one hand went up...then another, and soon all the hands within the company were in the air. Keeping my head down, without looking up at Peterson, an air of innocence I continued to pack my sea-bag trying not to draw attention. Careful not to show too much guilt, my grin was uncontrollably cracking upon my face.

It's time for the next phase of training, our designation schools. Mine was Computers. Automated Data Processing was to be my job in the big fleet. I had taken Carl's advice. Computers were a good option and I was eager to learn my trade.

Upon arriving at our new barracks, we settled in. These barracks had carpet and even ceramic tile in the bathrooms. Glass paned windows and separate cubicles with bunks and even a stand up locker with drawers, plenty of storage for my uniforms and "civvies". The Taj Mahal compared to the sparse accommodations of boot camp barracks. Sleep was the first order, and after that finding anything to eat other than galley food. Tiffalo and I were exhausted. I didn't know if I could have survived another week in boot camp. Awakened on a Saturday morning after an entire evening of twelve hour sleep I made my way into the showers. Turning the hot water handle, a steady stream of steaming hot water flows upon my face. Steam bellows up from the floor and I just melt into the experience. Taking my time without a company commander barking to hurry up. A "Hollywood" shower if you will, more military lingo that had now carved its' way into my vocabulary. Having lost several pounds in boot camp, my cravings for pizza, Kentucky fried chicken and peanut butter and chocolate ice cream from the 31 flavors ice cream shop on base were soon to be satisfied. Fat, cholesterol, and junk food binges were welcome vices. I gorged myself on everything. Extra crispy recipe, with a side of coleslaw then polished off with ice cream for desert and a large Slurpee. My cravings were unquenchable.

With our new freedom from the confines of boot camp, the next craving was discovering San Diego in true sailor's fashion. Sitting in the barracks lounge, eating that peanut butter and chocolate ice cream, other students had mentioned an area of San Diego that catered to sailors. Seaman Tiffalo pauses from puffing his cigarette and eavesdrops on their conversation. The red light district, Rosecrans Boulevard, famous for catering to squids and jarheads, plenty of temptations to go around for the big fleet. Of course this was the school where most of us would learn many lessons. Lessons that would contribute to a sailor's outlook while visiting exotic destinations like drinking plenty of booze, and blowing your paycheck on women. The college of debauchery.

"Let's go check it out Torres," said Tiff. The ladies thought was handsome with the look of Rhett Butler in Gone with the Wind. All the girls liked him. Knowing his track record it was hard to refuse the invitation. Being that I was a guy of average looks and kind of skinny, hanging around with Tiff increased my chances for more interaction or any action for that matter with the opposite sex, keeping in mind of course I still had a girlfriend back home. So it was on to Rosecrans for a little training not mentioned in our blue jackets manual.

Not really a big drinker or smoker and really didn't have much experience indulging in the seedy side of things. I was a party novice. Maybe a few late nights at the Goober Theatre, an X rated drive in somewhere off the beaten path outside Dothan Alabama. This experience because of a few high school dates with a girl that had a, well let's say a questionable reputation. But that was it. I was nervous to be an 18 year old kid out in a big town with a few sailors that had just graduated boot camp. But the thrill of the unknown outweighed the nervous stomach. So we marched on to the red light district of Rosecrans boulevard.

Bright lights and big city, flashy signs of porn shops, strip joints and 25 cent peep shows lined the street. Cheap motels and short skirt hookers under their flickering lights were also in the mix, a lot to take in. I was about to take my first steps into the underworld dressed in a cracker jack uniform and Dixie cup, very naïve. Bar to bar we drank a beer or two at each trying to look worldly and sophisticated. I kept up with each beer, trying to outdo Tiff and the others that came along, plenty of paychecks to blow.

No bills, no kids, no medical concerns, a dry bed at the barracks and three meals a day were the guarantee of being in the military. What else did I have to spend money on except for booze and dropping tips into g-strings? As the night turned into morning and having classes to attend by 8 a.m. on Monday we stumbled back to the base leaving a few of our stomach contents along the way.

Working hard and playing hard only two more months of late nights, hangovers and dropping dollar bills into several g-strings at Rosecrans we all attended our classes dutifully preparing to join the fleet. Having had a birthday, 19 years old by now my experience in the Navy was growing, all with good memories and some not so good. My friends celebrated my nineteenth birthday in true sailors' fashion. Renting a cheap motel room on Rosecrans and they invited the class to come and celebrate. Booze of all sorts stacked in rows on the dresser and strippers shaking their money makers for plenty of drunken sailors' tips. The little motel room was rockin'. Of course being the man of the hour my dances were free and so was the booze. We partied until the wee hours of the morning until finally the strippers were finished dancing and I was passed out in the bathtub. My world was expanding, a learning experience to say the least.

Luckily we all graduated from our schools and were anxious to learn of our fate in the fleet. The orders were announced as we all walked to the podium and took our envelope that disclosed each of our fates. "Groton

Connecticut" shouted the administrator as one lucky sailor would rise and take the orders at the podium with a big grin. "San Francisco" and again another sailor would rise and receive orders as their names were announced. "San Diego" more smiles. Then it came to my orders. "Torres...USS Proteus...Guam". Huh?...having nearly crapped my dress whites, where the hell was Guam? After all of the orders were handed out to the class, Tiff and a few others of my classmates gathered around a large world map that was pinned to the back wall. All looking for those countries or areas of the world they would be stationed. Guam, Guam...hmmm where is Guam we were all trying to find it on the map. Finally, Tiff exclaimed," here it is!" A pin prick in the Pacific Ocean in the middle of nowhere, on the other side of the world is where I would spend the next three years. Guam, my new home, would become known amongst the sailors stationed there as "The Rock".

Our professional training was over and I have known Tiffalo for nearly six months now. A friendship had grown but it was now time to once again salute and say goodbye. He was headed to a supply ship in San Francisco. Taking his orders and packing his sea bag, he closes the door to his locker. "It's been cool Torres" With tears welling up, his heart heavy, we both know this was the last time we'd see each other. Without a word he hugs my neck and leaves the barracks. Our shared experience and the private hell of boot camp we both endured, was a lifelong bond. The last friend from boot camp and amongst the guys I flew in with had finally said goodbye. "Fair Winds and Following Seas, Torres", He turned and faded into anonymousness.

Chapter 2

A RUSTY PIG

"All those sitting in rows A through F please board the plane now", was the announcement over the plane's cabin intercom. The courteous flight attendant of Continental Airlines smiled as she read the computer screen. I looked over my ticket, and surprised, "hey that's me", I thought. I presented my ticket and boarded the plane. To my surprise, I had first class! Maybe a mistake I thought, or maybe the guilt of sending me to Guam the Navy was taking pity on me. No not a chance of that. Probably a mistake but I'm not going to complain. Itinerary: 13 hour flight from San Francisco International with a layover in

Honolulu for fuel sounds good to me. So I settled in and took the pillow from the attendants hand and peered out the window.

As I sit peering out the window, "You got the window seat", a voice proclaimed. I look over and the person sitting next to me for the flight is putting up his overhead luggage. Removing his sports jacket, with elbow patches, a conservatively dressed middle aged man is peering down his gold rimmed glasses at me. "I always like getting the window, How are ya doin' sailor?" He noticed I was in my tropical dress white uniform. "Goin' to Pearl" he asked. "Not quite" I replied. "The name is Ted" extending his hand to introduce himself. "Good to meet ya…I'm Charlie". Ted settles into his seat and removes his glasses wiping the lenses. The rest of the passengers' board and flight attendant latches the door shut. The plane begins to taxi down the runway. "Well let's see what this thing will do" Ted said. The plane builds speed down the tarmac and off we go.

The plane levels off and the seat belt light blinks off, "So where you headed Chuck?" Ted asks. I kind of give a little chuckle with a blush to my face embarrassed I reply "Ever hear of Guam?" He chuckles "You mean the island?" as he orders up a couple of Whiskey sours from the attendant. "Well let's have a toast to your new command". Apparently the uniform is a form of i.d.

that should suffice for ordering alcohol for a now 19 year old kid. Between the enlisted men's club in San Diego, Rosecrans Boulevard and Ted I'm learning the art of drinking quite quickly. Of course the flight is somewhat long and after dinner and a drink, desert and accompanying liquor, casual drinks afterward Ted's conversation became indiscernible. He calls the attendant and orders another round, "One more of these" tapping on his empty glass. The attendant becomes concerned at his splashy speech and cuts him off from any more alcohol. During the flight and sloshy conversation, I learn Ted is a reporter for one of the big networks and is flying to location on a story. I also learn Ted is an alcoholic and he freely admits it once his addiction is exposed. Ted then has a request for his new flight friend, me. That is to order more drinks and keep them coming for him, and pass them off as my own. Why not? It is first class and all the drinks are on the house. Ted and I became buds. The seat belt lights flicker on and the captain comes onto the intercom, "We're arriving into Honolulu for a fuel stop and then onto Guam, Thank you for flying Continental". Ted and I buckle up and sip down our last bit of booze and the attendant collects our cups. The plane enters Honolulu airspace and lands. "Well this is where I get off" said Ted. "See ya Ted and good luck with your story". "Uh yeah, Chucky, yeah…uh thank you. You see my glasses Chuck?" checking his coat pockets and seat pouch he notices he's wearing them. "Uh o.k. here they are…" Ted murmurs. Gathering his things he stumbles off the plane into anonymousness. I have realized during my time in this canoe club, that is the Navy, that relationships with people are memorable and brief. You meet people, have shared experiences and in a short time they are saying goodbye and your paths part, typical in a military career.

The plane is refueled and my head is buzzing from all the drinks. I wonder what Guam is going to be like. The plane is eventually refueled and inspected and it's off we go again. This time I use that pillow quite extensively. The alcohol has created that hung-over haze that only sleep can cure. I sleep like a baby waking in brief moments to shuffle my ass and fluff my pillow. The flight seems to last forever. Then that angelic voice I've waited for, "Sir…Sir, we're about to land". The attendant awakens me and out the window the lights of a tiny island appear.

Landing on Guam in the wee hours of the morning, five o'clock a.m., standing there at baggage claim my sponsor is waiting. Dressed in floral shorts and flip flops a young, energetic and clean cut sailor from the ship is waiting. "I thought you were never going to make it". "You're an hour late. I was thinking you went AWOL"

(Absent without Leave). "I'm Seaman Rand, your sponsor". Sponsor, I had no clue what that meant. It's apparently a person assigned to new arrivals to greet them at the airport and get them settled into the new command. "Let's go and get your sea bag and get out of here. We'll stop at my place. My wife will have breakfast for us." I shake his hand and hope he doesn't notice my alcohol saturated breath.

The drive from the airport presents an opportunity to take in the surroundings. Peering from the window, the sunrise begins to peak above the horizon. "You can roll that down if you want," Rand said pointing at the window. "Sure," I replied, rolling down the hand crank. The moist and humid air of Guam flows into the open window. Large banana leaf palm trees line the little boulevards and coconuts dot the ground. The smell of sea air and little morning dew drops peck my face from the breeze of the open window. I see restaurants and bars, several massage parlors and strip joints along the streets as the sun rises and the street lights flicker off. Some of the signs of the shops are written in Chinese and Japanese. I realize I've entered a foreign world. We must be getting closer to the bases. Up another hill and down a few side streets we arrive at a little wooden house with a flower garden. "Let's get in and get some food. I'll get ready." Rand said. Greeted at the door by his wife

Pamela and his little girl Jesse, I settle into the squishy couch. "Are you hungry?" she asks. "Sure," I reply. I take off my Dixie-cup hat and sit down at the table for coffee and scrambled eggs. Rand enters the room half dressed in his dungarees and enjoys the meal. "Can I get freshened up?" I ask.

After grabbing a bite to eat, brushing my mucky teeth and alcohol soaked tongue, I thank Pamela for a nice meal and wait outside in Rand's little red Toyota. A hand-me-down "Guam Bomb" a name affectionately given to old cars sold from sailor to sailor. Rand emerges from his front door with spit shined boots, neatly ironed dungarees and a perfectly folded and formed Dixie cup. "Let's get to your new home Torres", Rand said with a grin. "I can't wait" I replied with an air of hopeful anticipation. I was curious to see my new ship, the USS Proteus.

Rand's little red Toyota sputters to the entrance of the ship row with all the supply ships and support ships for the 7th fleet, Polaris Point. Berth upon berth of neatly parked ships with shiny new paint jobs of Haze Grey, the standard color for naval vessels. Rand presents his base pass to the sentry upon stopping at the gate entrance. The sentry smiles as he waves the little red car through the gate. Peering out the window, at these newly painted ships I ask "Is it this one?"... "No" said Rand it's a little

farther down. "How about this one here on the left?"…
"No, a little farther down," said Rand. The little red car begins to slow to a gravel parking area and pulls in. Gravel crackling under the tires the car sputters to a stop.

In the near distance is a large dry dock. Within the dry dock, sits a huge steel hulk on large wooden blocks is a pitiful rust bucket of a ship being painted with a patch work of primer red. Welding torches spark in different areas around the decks, and sections of the ship's hull were being cut away. Other sections are being serviced. Scaffolding and other construction materials were scattered about the decks. A 20 foot shipping container was being used as a Project manager's office with a small window air conditioner dripping on the ground. Hard hats covered men and sailors with walkie-talkies coordinate the activity. Tired, filthy and exhausted sailors ending their 12 hour shifts were emerging from the dry dock. A far off exhausted gaze expresses their dirty faces. Their hands blackened by hard work, boots soiled and dusty they plop their feet with every step toward a barracks for a hot shower and sleep.

Rand slams the door to his little red Guam Bomb and he gets out. "Grab your sea bag Torres". Puzzled I continue to look around as if my ship is somewhere close but I can't see it. Poor souls I thought, the silence breaks. "There's your ship Torres" Rand exclaims. Rand pointing to the rusty pig in the dry dock, a surreal realization comes over me. "This?" I reply with a glimmer of fading hope that somehow Rand could be mistaken. "Yep, Welcome to the Pig" said Rand grinning with a deviant smile. I guess he understands what was going through my mind. And as many times in a few weeks I nearly crap my pants. "Let's get you to division," Rand said. An empty feeling fills my stomach, even after the breakfast I just ate. I couldn't get my mind wrapped around this picture of the rusty pig there in the dry dock.

The USS Proteus AS-19, a 40 year old nuclear submarine tender in dry dock for overhaul, keel laid in 1941 and completed in 1944. This ship was so old it was in Tokyo Bay for surrender day after WWII. A picture of the ship in Tokyo Bay on that day graced the ship's lounge.

Rand and I plod up a set of metal steps through a labyrinth of hoses, electrical cords, rope and other materials used for the overhaul, and up through a gang plank into the belly of the main deck. Thick welding fumes permeate the air. Welders, workers, laborers toil away like busy ants. Dirty overalls and dungarees are the standard uniform of the sailors assisting in the overhaul. Careful not to soil my whites, we continue to walk through the maze of passageways to the division to check in. Finally coming to a small door with a window, in we go, a brightly lit space with perfect blue paint, air conditioning and the smell of freshly brewed coffee. The first words I hear, "Is this the new guy?" Chief Wilson said. Chief Wilson, the divisional chief in charge of operations of the Automated Data Processing department for the ship. Rand, "Here he is all new and shiny". "Let's get him out of those whites and into dungarees." said the Chief. "He's got a big day in store. Get him checked into personnel and into the B.Q. (Basic Quarters/Barracks)." The crew was being housed in barracks during the overhaul. I shook a few hands and it is back walking through the maze of passageways for checking into personnel. Rand explained along the way the different areas of the ship, "This is the galley (chow hall), this is the crane boom, this is the crew's lounge" All of those areas that could be of use or importance during my stay onboard he toured and explained their function. Even battle stations for drills and chemical weapons attack stations. Let's not forget this is a military ship, very overwhelming and intimidating if you let it. I had a lot to learn. The surprises were not over.

Once checked into the Barracks on the base it was back to the ship the following day. In fresh dungarees, bell bottom jeans and a blue cotton button up shirt, I find my way back to the ADP department to begin my work in my chosen field...computers. Looking around the division and asking questions about what shift I'll be on the other sailors in the division politely showed me around. Rand was busy at work doing a series of steps for processing reports. He seemed very proficient with what he was doing. The other sailors would ask him questions which he seemed to know every answer to. So I decided to ask a few questions for myself. "So, Rand, what shift will I be on?" Rand, "Oh, you don't start here yet…here in division". "What do you mean?" I said. "Well", Rand went on to explain, "when you are new to a command you have to do collateral duties first then you'll be placed in your division once you complete that". Something the recruiter failed to mention. "So, what are these collateral duties?" I asked. "Come on," said Rand. After putting the finishing touches on what he was doing we leave the ADP department. Again through the maze of passageways up to an area near the front of the ship, we arrive at a dirty hatch, covered with soot and handprints. We turn the large squeaky lever to the hatch and enter into a black and gloomy dungeon of a space. Long drawn faces of tired and sooty sailors sitting around with CO_2 fire bottles and fume respirators draped around their necks.

"Here we got another one for ya", said Rand. First Class Petty Officer Litrell was at his little wooden desk. Dirty, finger-smeared work orders and tickets were in organized piles on the desk. Desk drawers broken off their tracks, Litrell struggles with the clumsy drawer until it succumbs to his shaking, opening it, he trifles through the junk trying to find a pen that works. Clicking each one and testing the ink with scribbles on one of the work orders he hands me the pen, "You'll need this" said Litrell. "Just note what time the job started and what time the job ended in these areas here". Litrell points to the blank sections on one of the work orders. Rand, "Well this is where you'll be for the next few months. What is Littrell 90 days or so?". "You're kidding me?!" I said. Litrell, "No kid, I have you for 90 to 120 days in the fire watch division until the refurbishment is done. We're short on manpower". I'm going to need new dungarees because for as many times in as few weeks, you guessed it, I nearly soiled myself again. "Let me know if you need anything else o.k.?" said Rand. Rand begins to turn and leave, "Thanks?"…I retorted sarcastically. Follow orders, Follow orders and keep your tongue I thought. My private hell was getting better and I really began to wonder if I had made the correct choice in my life path.

So for the next 4 months the "Pig" was welded, refitted, replaced and we all did our duty for the old seabird. As the weeks passed, I assisted welders on their jobs, dutifully writing in the start time and stop time of every work ticket. Providing much needed fire watch services in case the welders accidentally caught something aflame. Up and down the ladders into the catacombs and holes deep within the pig, the fire watches sailors toil away. Twelve hours on Twelve hours off, seven days a week. I had become one of those tired sailors I noticed leaving the ship on my first day. My face grimaces lugging around a 60 pound CO_2 fire extinguisher up and throughout the ship. Once even underneath the twenty thousand ton vessel. Under the belly as it rested upon large wooden supports watching my welder patch holes from under the ship a twenty-thousand ton vessel rests above my head. My fresh dungarees had become worn and blackened, soot stained rags, far from a regulation uniform. Short tempers became common amongst the fire watchmen as the days clicked on and on.

The countdown to work in ADP was nearing as the refit of the old pig was coming to an end. I had counted the experience in fire watch as an opportunity to learn the ship inside and out. I had been to places on that ship that not even the captain has seen. Deep within the boilers and bilges, under the belly and far forward in the deepest storage holds. From the engine room to the pilot house, I had seen it all. Good knowledge to have if ever there was an occasion to use it. I was looking forward to some time off and working in cleaner conditions. So I thought.

The crew had begun moving onboard their newly refitted ship. With newly painted bulkheads and tiled floors, fresh bedding and mattresses for all the racks and plenty of air conditioning. The plumbing in all the heads (bathrooms) was working correctly. It was almost time for sea trials and I was looking forward to moving to my division to work within the rate that I had chosen and also signed an additional year of enlistment for. I had only a few days left until my fire watch days were over. I threw away the old tattered dungarees and bought new ones in anticipation of the change in duties. New boots with spit polish shine and freshly ironed shirt I reported to ADP once my chains in the fire watch division had been cut. "Torres, we need you to report to the galley for "crankin" said Chief Wilson. "Huh? Crankin what's crankin?" I said. All new crew has to crank before their first cruise, and since the crew was now living onboard. I couldn't believe it. Another 3 months of mess duty awaited me. Follow orders, Follow orders. And yes I nearly soiled those new dungarees. Crankin' of course is how it sounds. Trying to feed a crew of 2000 sailors 3 meals a day takes quite a bit of resources and manpower. Up at four o'clock in the morning and not going to bed until around eight o'clock each night, believe me, after 16 hours of crankin' 7 days a week you're ready to go to bed at eight o'clock at night. From breakfast to dinner and lunch in between a "crank" as we who were "crankin" were referred to, washed pots and pans, prepared meals, cleaned large mixing vats, carried heavy boxes of meat, potatoes and veggies, eggs and cooking supplies to the mess cooks to make meals and stock out the refers. Those new dungarees soon became a disgusting stained painting of splashed on gravy and rotten eggs, mixed with sweat and dish soap, so much for buying the new dungarees. The shiny new boots splashed with every form of muck, mustard and potato peels you can imagine. If you were lucky you were put on the midnight shift to strip and wax the mess decks to a glossy shine ready for inspection daily. Those floors on the mess decks were as shiny as mirrors. But the price was back breaking strip waxing and buffing. Another level of the private hell I was living. I looked forward to that first cruise and this time, I was determined to finish these extra duties and work with computers. I still had faith.

Chapter 3

"THE ROCK"

By this time I had finished my collateral duties, "crankin" and fire watch. I had been on the ship 9 months and am now living a somewhat normal experience. Seaman Rand had been promoted and finished his tour on Guam. The ship was getting the final touches of the overhaul after sea trials and was being prepared for her newest voyage into the sea. So it was now time to discover this little island and what it had to offer.

Guam, acquired after the Spanish/American war liberated in WWII by American Marines this 20 mile long by 7 mile wide-island in the middle of the South

Pacific is an American Territory. War memorials and rusty battle guns dot the landscape. Reminders of the bloodshed of the battles fought against the Japanese by the Americans to retake the island invite you to stop and take pause of the sacrifice. Beautiful scenery, craggy rock coastlines, waterfalls, and hillside views of little villages depicts Guam's scenic beauty. Saltwater as clear as gin, great for every salt water activity known to modern man. Sunken Japanese warships provide an artificial reef for Scuba diving, fishing. Boating, swimming, you name it Guam has these great outdoor opportunities. Our group of ADP division sailors would soon learn what it has to offer.

Don, an upstate New Yorker and Buffalo Bills fan, cocky 2nd class petty officer was our unofficial leader. Married to a wonderful girl Bonnie, who was in the Navy as well were stationed together on Guam, she with a shore duty billet and Don on the pig. Don certainly tried to balance the responsibility of his wife and rank with a ragamuffin group of degenerates with a pension for irresponsible behavior.

Timbo, a Data Systems technician (repairs computers) from Louisiana was a smart and resourceful person. He found many new ways within his calculating and sometimes twisted mind to experience the many temptations available to us in those exotic ports.

Dave, a midwest dairy farmer from Wisconsin, smoked Marlboro lights like they were going out of style and would try anything on a dare, had a liver that could digest copious amounts of alcohol.

Jonnie, a kid around my age, from a small town in Maine, Heavy New England accent became my best friend. Always increasing the stakes with every dare or challenge, of how far we could push the envelope of debauchery, would find a new low with every trip off base.

William, Jose', and Dennis from Boston were others that rounded out our little group.

They and I shared many experiences on Guam, WestPac cruises and the ports that bonded us. Many of these experiences were on Guam. Working the evening shifts we usually left the ship after our shift was up and blew a few bucks in the little drinking holes around the island and became my lifelong brothers.

Mi Elana's Lounge, Uncle Bob's Watering hole, and Barney's at the Beach for the annual coconut Olympics were our favorite Guamanian hang outs. Filling our bellies full of beer and liquor shots, we all tried to keep up with those seasoned sailors that had a professional drinking license. This is where we met one of our newest mates, "Boy Wonder" aka William. A young heavy metal kind of kid that loved banging his head to heavy riffs of

Metallica. New to the ship and trying to make friends, "Boy Wonder" earned his name by challenging us to drinking until we drop. Unfortunately this 18 year old fresh out of boot camp kid didn't know what he signed up for with this challenge. Once finished with our drinking binge for the night we all went to the parking lot outside Mi Elanas and Will decided that his stomach needed a reprieve from the power shots slammed within our little watering hole. Power puking like a four inch fire hose, high velocity and well chunked, Will earned his new nickname, bestowed upon him by Don, "The Boy Wonder" mocking his ability to hang. This name stuck for the remaining time onboard.

Our little group of friends explored many corners of that island. From the north tip to Talofofo falls we hopped every bar and watering hole in between.

All bonding experiences while discovering this little island created our sense of comrade, not to mention fighting the local residents on a regular basis. The native population of Guam consists of Chamorro Indians that have an axe to grind with the government and a chip on their shoulder against military personnel that dwell upon their precious island. You've seen this kind of native in the old sailing movies. You know the ship's launch reaches the beaches of a tropical sandy shore and the sailors get out and look around. The bushes then part and the natives peek out with wide eyes, spears and shrunken head necklaces draped around their necks. This is the overall impression I was left with from some of the natives of Guam, very hostile attitudes towards sailors. Whether jealousy or just plain hatred, the experiences on this island with the natives, created a sense of paranoia amongst the military personnel stationed there. It made me pity the sense of loss of respect for the memory of their ancestors that were murdered by the Japanese, and the blood shed by American servicemen that gave them back their freedom. I had begun to discover my appreciation for my freedom.

Chapter 4

UNCLE BOB'S BRAIN HEMORRHAGE

Uncle Bob's Watering Hole, an open air saloon with pool tables and a large projection television, drink prices were cheap and the lonely Navy wives loved to dance. Playing pool and watching the animated movie "Heavy Metal" on the projection screen the place was packed. The "Boy Wonder" and I approach the bar. The bartender is bragging about his new concoction, The "Brain Hemorrhage". A shot glass filled with peach schnapps with a drizzle of bailey's Irish cream. The Irish cream, if curled right, will appear as a floating brain within the schnapps. And a drop of grenadine for the hemorrhage finishes off the look of the "Brain Hemorrhage".

Racking the pool tables and playing round after round "Boy Wonder" was a pro. No one could knock him off the table. But after a few Brain Hemorrhages his play began to waiver. Looking back at the movie screen and singing the words of the songs to the sci-fi animated flick, our minds were becoming affected by the bartender's new drink. "O.k. Charlie, let's go again", and another Brain Hemorrhage went down the hatch. The "Boy Wonder" was challenging me again with a drinking binge. He finally loses our pool table and the movie draws to the end, our minds are swimming with baileys and peach schnapps.

After several brain hemorrhages, and near empty pockets, The "Boy Wonder", and I completely waxed, found our way back to the ship. I crash into my rack head swirling in the wee hours of the morning. Suddenly awakening to find myself trying to escape the space between the wall and my rack, about 8 inches wide. How in the hell did I get back here I wondered. In an instance of half-drunk realization I begin to power puke brain hemorrhages all over the berthing space walls, coating them with baileys and peach schnapps. Slithering out from the wall and rack like a baby snake trying to escape its shell, simultaneously, "Boy Wonder" thrust back the curtain to his rack, leaned his head over the third tier of his rack and let's go the brain hemorrhage goo that was occupying his stomach. Power spraying all over the berthing walk way. Waking the other ship mates within the berthing, laughter from disbelief of the vomiting orchestra echoed throughout the space. Dave, Johnny and the others come to our rescue.

Dragging both "Boy Wonder" and me to the showers, our friends twist on the cold handle for an icy cold shower to de-puke us. The icy water shocks me awake to see my friends laughing faces. The "Boy Wonder" threatens to kick everyone of their asses between vomit heaves as they turn up the velocity of the water continuing to mockingly laugh as the cold water soaks us down.

Tucked back into our racks in vomit soaked sheets, the berthing space becomes quiet again until the next morning. The Boy Wonder and I were rudely awakened by the divisional first class Lang. Lang shouts us awake, "Get into your uniforms and come with me!" shaking and barking the Boy Wonder and I into sobriety. After getting our brains operational we plod along the breezeways with Lang to get large metal buckets and mops to clean the berthing area. Talk about regretting the night before, every speck of partially digested chow that was painted along the walls and deck of the berthing space had to be scrubbed to inspection quality. Sponges and puke soaked rags stopped up every nasty bit of those brain hemorrhages. Wipe and rinse, wipe and rinse, never have I regretted experimenting with a new drink than I did that day or any day since.

Not learning any lessons from Boy Wonder and my mistakes my shipmates and friends continued the same drinking binges on many occasions. Mi Elanas, our home away from the ship was notorious for late night binge drinking amongst our little group.

While driving back to the ship one evening from Mi Elaina's, Wayno (another friend), Jonnie and myself just past the main gate to Polaris. With Wayno driving me at shotgun and Jonnie seated behind me, Jonnie exclaims, "Pull Over!" Wayno, "You can't make it to the ship?" not slowing down at all. Jonnie, "No, I'm not kidding…" Suddenly the ominous familiar gurgle and spew was heard from Jonnie. And of course, Jonnie decides that I need a shower. A warm shower of booze and stomach acid was power sprayed upon the back of my head. A vomit shampoo if you will. Jonnie never knew that he had a future in hair care and neither did I. Wayno finally pulls over at a small picnic area near the ship's berth that opens up to a small beach into the Apra Harbor. Jonnie spills out from the back seat of Waynos' car onto the sandy parking area. Fully clothed Johnnie and I had a date with the salt water harbor to wash away the vomit.

Shark infested and during evening feeding times for the Pacific reef shark we brave the cold salty plunge. Dunking my head and washing the vomit from my hair, Jonnie up to his shoulders washing away the muck from his clothes we got back to the car and onto the ship. Walking up the gang plank and onto the Quarter deck Wayno, Jonnie and I, sopping wet and dripping, salute the Officer of the Deck. "Request permission to come aboard sir"... "What the hell happened to you?' He replies. "We went swimming". "Granted", he replies with a scowl. Looking back, the sight of soaking wet sailors standing on the Quarterdeck baffles me that we were allowed to come aboard at all.

Fist fights on the weekends added to the adventure a young sailor could experience. On several occasions ending up with a black eye, or broken hand from punching people. Busted knuckles from someone's teeth, cut eyebrows I can't count. The weekend brawls at the local watering holes with the natives seemed inevitable. Nearly bitten by a mangy dog one of the locals threatened to unleash this animal upon me and my friends. Pulling into the parking lot of Barney's, a group of Chamorro locals gave us the hard looks of the intruders on their island. It was the annual coconut Olympics and we were there to take in the festivities so, not wanting any trouble we ignored the hard looks until, "Hey Haoli!

You park too close to my friend's car! If you don't move it I'm going to send this dog on you!" One of the locals shouted. Having had a belly full of this racist horse shit I couldn't hold back, "Fuck you asshole! If you send the dog I'll kill the fuckin' thing!" I shouted back. My buddies readied for what was about to occur as the locals standing from the seats within the truck and coming out to meet us. Removing the dog from the back of his dented up pickup truck he unleashed the barking animal at us. Whap! I gave a kick that would make any football field goal kicker proud, the biting dog ran yelping down the street, and we began to teach this crazy local and his pals a few lessons in etiquette. Dave smacks the biggest one with his Wisconsin cheese fed fist and he falls flat on his face. The rest of us pick an opponent and begin to take out our bruised egos on the loud assholes. It was unusual these guys would try to take us on one on one. The locals would usually wait until there was only one or two of you and ten of them when they would decide to have the "bravery" to confront us. This gave us a negative impression about Guam hence the nickname… "The Rock". Of course in this instance, we prevailed. Once the tussle in the parking lot was over and the locals piled back into the beat up truck and drove off, it was our time to get our coconut cups filled with bullfrog. Bullfrog, a lime flavored wedding punch with light rum and fruit chunks the chosen beverage to ease our injured egos. Of course some of the guys would always choose beer. We settled in to Barney's sandy floors and sand bar with coconut cups and bar snacks of spicy octopus chunks. Pieces of octopus tentacles hot soaked and cooked in pepper sauce and vinegar. These little chunks were actually quite good but a little chewy. The point though was to create thirst, and they certainly did that.

The events in the annual coconut Olympics were dancing sea hags. The fattest and sweatiest bellied guys in the place would don the coconut brazier and grass skirts and do the best hula as drunken servicemen, new to the island, had their faces buried in the sea hags' sweaty belly to extract a salty olive from their belly buttons. The winner received the loudest applause for the best sea hag, as the score was kept for each event and each contestant.

Next was the toilet paper roll exchange relay that needed the assistance of women. The women would hold the toilet paper rolls between their knees and the guys would take a wooden paper towel spindle between their knees and the relay began in earnest. The guys would scurry down the length of the relay track and insert the paper towel spindle into the roll of toilet paper and bring it back to the bucket. The most toilet paper rolls at the end in each bucket would be the winner.

The coconut shred was also an event. Each contestant would tear open and crack a coconut in its raw form and shred the meat from the coconut on a little chair with a shredding spoon attached. The most shredded meat at the end would win.

These events would become the staple of Barney's at the Beach. And especially at the end of the day when the medals were awarded, Barneys' treated all the patrons to the complementary wet t-shirt contest from the ladies entries. A good time had by all.

Of course the fight in the parking lot to begin our day left us with a sense of empty satisfaction. The military brass, realizing the cultural climate on Guam towards the military establishment, tried to create a sense of community by adopting sister villages for each ship. The ship would throw barbeques and get-togethers with the sister village in an effort to build bridges with the sailors, airmen and marines. The Proteus sister village was Santa Rita. The experience with the Santa Rita people was a positive one, so in fairness, I cannot condemn all the people of Guam for the negative actions of a few. It was these experiences that gave me hope that the Guamanian people would come to appreciate their unique history and relationship with the U.S. Military. A pig roast on the picnic grounds of Apra Harbor was scheduled one weekend. The people of Santa Rita and the sailors of the

Proteus enjoyed the cultural exchange. Diving platforms, swimming, balloons, and plenty of hamburgers, hot dogs and beer completed the day.

The pig roasted away with the villagers tending to its embers, the smell of roasted pig filled the air. Digging into the pig everyone had a tasty share of the pulled pork, nothing left but bones and fat except for the singed head. Ears folded from the heat of the embers, tongue curled and eyes turned pale gray, the head was all that really remained. One villager exclaimed, "The head is the best part!" Whether joking or not he kept a straight face and challenged Dave from Wisconsin to eat the brain. Dave, a dairy farmer and Green Bay Packers fan from Wisconsin had true grit. "I can handle anything," he said. The villager cracks open the now exposed skull of the baked creature and expose the fleshy gray matter steaming up through the open crack. Digging deep into the creature's head Dave plunges his fingers to the very bottom of the head cavity. Pulling out the half gelatinous and rubbery brain, it wiggles and splashes remnants onto the picnic table. We all wait and watch as Dave contemplates the attempt. Getting up his nerve, he takes a deep breath and stuffs the gob of gelatinous goo into his mouth, gives a few chews and swallows. With a few chirps and gurgles he keeps it down. The villager laughs, applauds and then discloses, "I've never seen that before, but you did it!" Dave, with a half smile realized he'd been had, gave a whimper of a chuckle with eyes watering, and slugs his beer hard to keep it all down. We all have a laugh at Dave's expense.

Camping trips on the beach, empty bottles of booze and passed out shipmates in the sand, we didn't realize how good we had it. Scuba diving in the clear gin waters around the island life abounds, anemones and sea turtles, sharks, turkey fish and crown of thorns, even old WWII wrecks, Guam's waters provided us refuge from the world outside. From the all-you-can-eat Mongolian barbeque joints to late night crashes at Don and Bonnie's place, our friendship had been sealed. Tan and sun baked we thought of the folks back home as we complained about our being so far away. Sipping coconut cups of "BullFrog" at Barney's and nibbling on spicy soaked octopus chunks, Guam, this rock in the middle of the Pacific, had become our home away from home.

Chapter 5

SUNSET AT SEA

Once settled onto the "Pig", my rack, a six foot by three and a half foot wide metal coffin, and thin 3 inch thick mattress with a hidden compartment underneath for storage, became my home. The Navy even threw in a little blue curtain for privacy. Everything I owned fit into these stowage compartments under my rack. Letters from my girl back home, candy, uniforms, civvies (civilian clothes), my graduation camera and a few other essentials. I carefully select the location of my rack amongst several others within the berthing compartment. A rack that is close to my friends and the hatch easy to find fumbling around in the dark after a long night of liberty.

A sailor's rack is his home on board a ship, his personal domain which is respected by all. This little corner of privacy is sacred ground for reading, writing letters, sleeping and re-leaving the pangs of young men at sea. And believe me after being at sea for several weeks it is a realistic activity. The "boys" get blue, especially for a ship full of young sailors whose average age is less than twenty-five.

The Proteus is ready for open water and the crew is busy preparing the ship for her next voyage into the Western Pacific (West Pac). A Western Pacific cruise usually consists of working ports mixed with liberty ports in the far east orient and sometimes Australia. Cruising through the South China Sea, Sea of Japan, and Pacific waters a WestPac cruise is a unique experience. The stories of exotic ports from the veteran WestPac sailors abound as supply crews load large pallets of boxed food stuff onto large chain hooks hoisted onto conveyor belts and into storage holds. It's time to make for those exotic ports, Philippines, Japan, Hong Kong and Korea.

I must make one last phone call to the girlfriend back home before we set out. Walking into the base enlisted club for a beer, Andy's Pub, I wait to use the free phones. Andy's pub was just off the ship's berthing maybe two hundred yards or so. It had a little bar, phones to call home, and even a place to do laundry. I settle into a small booth and dial 13,000 miles and 5 time zones away. My heart is thumping as I'm dialing the numbers on the old rotary phone dial. The phone rings and picks up. It's Melanie. Immediately, I heard it in her voice. Timid and evasive, I knew what was coming. The girlfriend I had since high school finally had enough of the long distance relationship. Cologne laced letters just weren't cutting it anymore. She longed for my flesh and blood that she just could not get 13,000 miles away on the other side of the world. She had chosen to call an end to the long distance relationship and I didn't blame her. It was me who chose the Navy. The long voyages in the Western Pacific have just become lonelier.

Having arrived in March, I have been aboard the Proteus for several months and now finally in my division and the ship ready for sea. The whistle blows, the mooring lines are brought aboard and the tug boats are pushing the old pig out of her berth and into Apra Harbor away from Guam. A spanking new haze grey paint job with bright white S-19 lettering on the bow shines with perfection. The Proteus is finally underway. Don waved goodbye to Bonnie back on the pier as Jonnie, Timbo and me, rolled up the mooring lines as part of the line teams that man each heavy mooring station on the weather deck. We watch as the "Rock" slips into the distance. The group leaves back to the division and I stay on the weather deck and take in the sea. I had never experienced the sea past the beaches of Florida and for me it was a new experience.

This unique experience gave me a new appreciation for being in the Navy. It gave me time to reflect as did Griffith Park back in L.A. a place to consider all things and wonder about the future. The power of the sea pitching the ship up and down creating froth from the wake with each plunge of the bow, gave me pause to realize just how powerful the sea is. I had faith in the overhaul of the "Rusty Pig". Flying fish emerge from the seafoam of the wake and with pointed little fins like wings, skim the top of the water until out of sight. Brilliant sunrises, deep royal blue colors of the ocean, exotic and colorful fish, the sound of fog horns in the distance, and the salty taste of sea spray on your lips. In the early dusk I gaze upon a sunset of a harmonious blend of pinks and purples that turn into a rich hew of yellows and then to brilliant orange and eventually a velvet red sun diminishing behind the darkness of the pitch black ocean horizon. I sat and enjoyed each evening on the weather decks reading letters about my family and friends back home. As daylight diminished and the stars took over, the full spectrum of the universe, the blackness of the ocean night enveloped the Proteus, became too dark to read my letters. I managed to find the crew's lounge. Down from the weather decks two decks or so, just follow the smell of pipe tobacco and popcorn. Within the lounge, several off duty sailors played poker, smoking endless cigarettes to contribute to the mountain of ashes accumulating in each available ashtray. Of course old movies playing on the closed circuit television system keep the boredom away, a place of refuge from the close quarters of shipboard living, or when not standing watch.

Of course the ship was a naval vessel which commanded the entire attention of the crew when on duty. Standing watch in the open bridge, my job was to be a telephone talker relaying orders from the officer of the deck for navigation and combat training, a critical and stressful position to say the least.

Wobbly legged sailors that haven't gotten their sea legs yet, seasick and leaving their vomit in the stairwells, a vile mixture of chow line food, and stomach fluid sloshes around the bottom of the stairs. The lack of privacy and the restriction of being on a ship for weeks on end, a sailor really looks forward to liberty call. Of course living with several other men in a confined space has its drawbacks, stinky socks and a quiet silence of the berthing compartment, broken by an occasional explosion of a fart with laughter from the guilty party to soon follow. Always a worry of catching crabs crawling from one bunk to another, from some poor unfortunate soul who decided to visit one of the massage parlors on Guam the night before deployment, these all part of shipboard life. Settling into the new life onboard the Proteus begins to train her crew for any contingency cruising on testing all of her crew and equipment to be battle ready. "General Quarters, General Quarters – all hands man your battle stations", the announcement over the 1M.C. Drilling the crew for battle was standard procedure, General attack, Chemical attack, Damage Control and Fire fighting training, Evasive maneuvers and communications training. Setting yoke and dogging the hatches for watertight integrity. Improvising solutions to flooding in a battle scenario are many drills to keep the crew ready for any situation in Ronald Reagan's six hundred ship navy. A very big fleet as the Soviet Union is still a threat. Day in and day out, the drills and military stress continues until relief of this daily monotony comes in the form of a "Steel Beach Picnic".

Steel beach picnic is a term for a ship board function that takes place on the helo-deck (helicopter deck). Lawn chairs and blankets strewn across the Helo-deck in a beach side fashion for off duty sailors to lie about. Mess deck cooks grill hot dogs and hamburgers for the crew while the crew catch a few rays of sun in an attempt to tan their pale hides. Pale from being inside a ship for weeks sometimes without going outside depending on where your watch was. So the steel beach picnic was a welcome break. Relaxing, the veterans of previous Westpac cruises flap their gums of sea stories already experienced while we cook on the hot steel deck. "Yes, the Philippines have so many girls", said one vet. "It's the last unspoiled paradise, you know naked girls all over the beach, hot night clubs and cheap beer." Jonnie, Don and Timbo all look at each other as the stories from the vets are almost unbelievable. Girls, booze, debauchery in its most unadulterated forms all seemingly chalked up to another sea story. Jonnie and I consider all the options.

We realize the vet may not be exaggerating, especially when corpsmen from the medical department, begin to push around a large metal mop bucket full of condoms. The basic condom, Trojan non-lubricated non-ribbed, the basic government issued no frills ride raincoat. It then dawned upon us that our port was within a few more days' cruise and we should take advantage of the free "advice" the corpsman was giving out. Jonnie and I reach into the mop bucket and take a handful or two of the sailor's best friend. After sailing and drilling for a few weeks the message is relayed that we are heading to the Philippines for a few weeks' liberty. Much needed after several weeks of hard core training. Arriving in the Philippine sea small islands begin to appear.

As dusk comes upon the Proteus, it snakes through the narrow Straits of Luzon, a tricky navigation through the craggy rock-laden shorelines of the Philippine Islands. Don, Timbo and Jonnie and I stare off the main deck rail anticipating the port may be around the next set of islands. We speak of all the stories the vet talked about at the steel beach picnic and wondered what stories we would have after this cruise. We all get so caught up in our conversation that we barely notice the little fishing vessels that are beginning to appear anchored near the rocky shores. More signs of human activity. Until out of the near darkness of the slowly setting sun, the lights of the port begin to illuminate. Could this be it? I thought. We all stared at the lights and began to realize we have made it. The port lights flickered from the biggest U.S. Naval base in the Pacific, Subic Bay.

Chapter 6

LIBERTY FOR THE CREW

The morning comes and the disbursing officer is exchanging American Dollars for Philippine Pesos on the mess decks. The clink and clank of little coins drop into a metal money box, each little compartment full to the brim with coins and colorful foreign money. Long lines of sailors with gobs of paycheck cash in hand from weeks at sea, snake around the corridors of the mess decks, 22 pesos for 1 American dollar. Jonnie and I do the calculations as we stand in line, "O.k. it's 8 pesos for one beer. That equals about 38 cents per beer. Approximately 3 beers for a dollar give or take. "So for about 5 bucks we'll have a good buzz going" Jonnie smiling as we look at our wads of cash saved up from a few paychecks at sea. The crew all chatted with grins of anticipated debauchery in the tiny clubs of Olongapo.

We feel the ship "bump" as it is getting moored alongside our berth on the pier. "It won't be long now" Jonnie said. The whistle from the intercom blows long and distinctive tune that all sailors come to know, and then the announcement over the intercom "Liberty for the crew." The sacred sentence has been spoken. Liberty, liberty, the time for rest and relaxation for well deserved and tired sailors from weeks of cruising and drilling has finally arrived. After exchanging our money, poke our heads from the mess decks into the morning air of the weather decks. Jonnie and I observe the first sight of Subic. The fleet is in. The Aircraft carrier USS Constellation from Japan and all her escorts are in port. Five thousand sailors on the carrier alone, plus a few hundred sailors per ship for all the escorts, the price of pussy just went up. Ships of all sizes from destroyers to frigates Subic is living up to its big reputation. Timbo, Jonnie, Don and I get in line for the quarterdeck, after the officers and chiefs of course, to strike down the gangplank and into our first port.

Walking to the main gate the smell of Olongapo, the town outside the base, distinctly permeates the air. As we near the main gate, policemen from the local station inspect our pockets for any contraband not allowed into the country. Of course flipping a couple of pesos to the policeman always gets things hurried along. Olongapo beckons. We leave the main gate of the base and onto a small bridge. The bridge spans the dirty banks of Shit River. Originally named the Kalaklan River, Shit River as it is nicknamed, is a river full of vile refuse of a Naval Base and a large Filipino town. It handles all of the sewage. Young boys bob and swim below as they yell to sailors, "Peso, Peso!" the sailors abide by tossing the heavy peso coins into the river. As the splash of the coins enters the water the boys dive below to retrieve the shiny coins. Bringing the coins up in their teeth, the boys waive and smile as sailors applauded the death defying feat. Crazy as hell! I thought. Or maybe just desperate, I thought I was deprived as a kid. It made baling hay look like a wonderful opportunity and I related to their desperation. I would not take any opportunity for granted again.

As we all enter the boulevard, Magsaysay, the street opens up into a plethora of neon signs, restaurants, hotels and nightclubs. Political posters dot the light posts and sides of buildings depict the overthrow of Ferdinand Marcos, the current president of the Philippines. A heartless dictator by some standards that lives in luxury while the citizens suffer in poverty, the political climate was precarious. Our group emerges into the night. Opening riffs of the rock song "Have a drink on me" by AC/DC are piped into the open air from heavy speakers outside Cal Jam, a large nightclub on the boulevard. So much to take in the sights, the sound and even the smell, sailors and marines choking down monkey meat on a stick and chicken feet from little corner barbeque grills set up on the boulevard. Street vendors with all sorts of wares, necklaces, t-shirts and ballut push their goods at you and demand money. "You buy now! Very good" they would say. Street walkers promising to "Love you for a long time". The street walker yells, "Don't be cheap Charlie me love you long time, just 200 peso." Of course we were warned about streetwalkers. If not working in a night club a streetwalker probably can't pass her health exam and have a "health card" to work, thus the risk of disease. So we politely decline the street walkers. Beggars and con men abound. Night club workers stand in the doorways and bark to gain our attention, little mom and pop shops with cruise jackets for sale. The people of Olongapo welcome the fleet. Our thoughts are racing as we have never been recognized as the big Americans before. The protectors of the free world have arrived or so I thought. I wondered if this is how the Romans felt, we the sailors of the seventh fleet in Reagan's six hundred ship Navy. Big powerful ships with professionally trained crews, anchored in such a small country. My ego was being fed and my head swelled as I had never been "popular" before, all fueled by plenty of pesos. I relished the attention. Sign upon neon sign of nightclubs, which one to choose. So as if flipping a coin we just picked one and entered... JB's Gallery of Girls.

JB's a small bar, but lined with bikini clad dancers, dancing upon a mirrored stage from one end to the next leaves little to the imagination. Loud music piping in from large speakers surrounding a DJ booth, mirrored walls and fluorescent lights, we sit down in a red leather booth and order a round. San Miguel Beer, the nationally produced beer of the Philippines. Ice cold, ice globs are stuck on the side of the bottle and resembles a candle with melted wax buildup oozing over the side. The coldest beer I've ever had. The first sip was cool and refreshing. I tilt the bottle back and enjoy the finest beer in the P.I.

Returning the bottle to the table I realize we all have some company. Four bikini clad LBFM's or Little Brown Fucking Machines, have magically materialized inside our booth. "Hey baby, you like" the dancer said. Her huge bosoms busting out of spaghetti strap bikini. For a 19 year old kid, I thought I had died and gone to heaven, plenty of girls, beer, money and a playground to play in. What else could you want? "Photo sir?" a voice nearby asks. I look over and a waiter with an instant camera waits... "Uh, no thanks man, not now." "Only 5 peso" the waiter pleads. "No thanks" I politely reply. Pictures too I thought. The tips to the dancers came and went as well as several dancers to our table and we thought well we're achieving one of our first goals of a sailor getting drunk but how about getting laid?. It's on to more clubs to sample the local scenery.

Cal Jam, short for California Jam, a large club with a steel dance floor with stairs of many levels, a more traditional nightclub with sailors, marines and their escorts for the night, all dancing to the DJ tunes being spun behind a large glass enclosure. And again more girls, photographers and ice cold San Miguel. We take in the atmosphere of the big pounding dance floor, spinning strobe lights and bikini clad honeys hopping onto our laps. Jonnie and I argue of which girl is sexier, "You have a boner yet?" Jonnie yells over the music. "I had a boner five minutes ago!" responding as my bikini girl rides my lap and presses her ample bosoms into my chest. Don dutifully shuns the girls as he is married shakes his head at me and Jonnie. Don staring and Jonnie and me having our fun with the women," This sucks. I wish we could see live music somewhere. You guys are having all the fun with these girls and I can't. Let's find a band". We ask around and sure enough, our little sailor's playground of

Olongapo has a live band night club, the "Apple Rock". We have a couple more beers and a few more dances and head to live entertainment. "I just got a boner and now we got to leave!" Reluctantly Jonnie slugs down the last ounce of his beer and it is on down the road to see some live entertainment.

We stumble out of Cal Jam and into the boulevard. Walking down broken sidewalks vendors clamor for us to buy their wares. Pushing through the throngs of 7th fleet sailors, girls and vendors, we see the sign, a large green neon apple protrudes from the building "APPLE ROCK". We enter what would become Don's favorite club. Inside, full dark red carpeting spans the floor, opens into a blackened dungeon of cigarette smoke and dozens of tables on a main floor, steps to a balcony level of tables. On the stage an all Filipino band ripping tunes from Black Sabbath and Motley Crue. After each number the crowd yelling out requests for the band to play. "Deep Purple!", "Ozzie", Jonnie yells out "Poison"… "Poison?" what the hell I thought. "Scorpions!" one yells out. Upon hearing a request the band strikes up their well used instruments to perform. Even in slightly broken English the band plays each song flawlessly. They're memorized song list seemed endless. Ice cold beer flows and the girls dance. My mind races with lust with each hit of my beer and the bounce and jiggle of the LBFM's bump and grind to the hit rock songs of the 1970's and 80's. Except for Don playing his air drums, the rest of us enjoy the company of the dancers. Out of the darkened and smoky silence the band begins to play the opening score of "Still Loving You", the Scorpions song that was a shouted out request.

The slow riffs begin and the tempo slows, the dancer's change their sway to meet the slow riffs. That's when I see her, standing out from the dancing girls gyrating and pumping on the platforms, Sari is pure exotic beauty. Long silky hair flows down thin shoulders to a perfectly arched back. Big brown eyes with puckered lips Sari is a diamond among gems. She dances in unison with the slow guitar riffs, long black hair caresses her every movement. I can't help but stare at her, she sees my hungry eyes. Slinking down the platform she steps down the stairs towards my mesmerized stare, like a cobra dancing for her victim. My lonely cruises without the thought of my girl back home begin to melt away. The riffs of the song build into the passion. Small beads of sweat glisten upon her back through the shimmering gleams of the mirror ball. Climbing onto my lap she pushes into me and the song takes us. We melt into passionate embraces as the song continues, Sari singing the words as she gyrates her half naked body against my blue jeans and t-shirt. The music swells and my mind is in a million places, half drunk and aroused from weeks at sea, I fall for the temptations of the last paradise on earth, "Pay my bar fine?" Sari gently whispered into my ear. Sure I thought. She takes my hand and leads me to a dark corner of the room. Sari, "Just talk to her and I'll be right back". Sitting in the corner of the bar the "Lady". Momma-san, dressed in a silky moo-moo, "Six hundred" momma-san says. I pay the six hundred peso bar fine, as the song dies down and the patrons applaud. Don puts the finishing beats on his air drums, Sari returns and has changed clothes from the bikini into her street clothes. The Momma-san wraps Sari's wrist with a band that emancipates her from the club. I leave the others to their own fate with Sari on my arm.

Walking out of the Apple Rock into the Olongapo night, Sari, "So what is your name?" I shyly reply. She doesn't seem to be the same seeing her in regular clothes. The allure of the night club has changed into this is just a regular girl. Not a working girl. But of course neither of us is under any allusions. Walking into the night of the lights and activity, Sari shows me the boulevard and the little nooks and crannies of Olongapo. Eventually the night wears on and a hotel room seems to be the next order of business. Sari picks one that she seems familiar with. We entered the little hotel. A musty smell of years of monsoon water saturation in the wood permeates the little hotel office.

Getting the keys we climb the wooden stairs to the second floor. The stairs have that hollow wooden sound of an old building. Entering the room it is certainly not the Hilton. A small double bed with metal tubes for a frame and window a/c, Sari checks the bathroom and the bed for cleanliness and then sets the temperature to the air conditioning unit in the window. "I'll just be a minute" she says as she departs into the bathroom.

Feeling a bit awkward, I get ready for bed and plop into the tightly tucked sheets. My heart thumping I've never done this before. Wow a girl in every port sure is not an exaggeration. Sari emerges from the bathroom, hair neatly brushed and tiny t-shirt, she gently enters the bed. I couldn't believe this experience. The stories I've heard from the steel beach vets are true. Sari is beautiful.

Donning the free advice from the corpsman at the steel beach picnic, I completed the second stage of a sailor's mission. The night becomes complete as the little window air conditioner clicks on to cool the room. Sari was unforgettable. I remember her name, but always wondered if she remembered mine. Then I realized this was little more than a business transaction to her. Little did I know that this was only the opening act to many memories to come, it is true there is a girl or several girls in every port, but there was much more to the Philippines that me and the boys were about to discover.

Late the next morning the division is on a skeleton crew, only two people per shift. We all happened to have 3 days of free time until our day to man the shop in ADP division. Grabbing a shower at the little hotel I say goodbye to Sari, giving her a tip for her efforts. She politely thanks me for the experience and disappears into anonymousness. I walk to a nearby barbeque spit and get a few sticks of monkey meat. Little bits of skewered monkey meat on a stick coated with spicy sauce and seared over a hot grill. Taking the chunks off the skewers with my teeth, I taste the delicacy. Spicy, chewy and a little dark tasting, the monkey meat gets me through the early morning hunger pangs as I pass on the chicken feet on a stick being offered up by the street vendor.

I hop into a trike, a small motorcycle with a sidecar, and head back to the ship for a change in clothes and more money. The little engine buzzes as the driver recklessly drives in and out weaving through traffic back to the main gate. I make it back to the ship alive. Back at my rack I change clothes and get a few more bucks for the days' activity. Several of the ADP sailors have already come and gone. Their cigarette smoke saturated clothes stuffed into their laundry bags hanging on wall hooks within the berthing compartment. Luckily lunch was being served on the mess decks and I grabbed a decent meal before I left again. Jonnie, Timbo racks are not touched as they are probably still in town. Don is sleeping and I leave him to his slumber. It's back in Olongapo I go.

Heading down the boulevard I come across another ship mate Dennis from Boston. Another New England accent but with a heavier draw. He said, "Hey there's this place called Barrio Baretto want to head up there?" I agree and it's off to the Baretto.

Dennis and I take a Jeep nee' up to the Barreto. It's about a 15 minute ride north of Olongapo, a little village setting with, of course, several little concrete block pubs and bars that line the main street. Not so neon but with brightly painted signs that catch your attention. Several little homes in the hills dot the hillside. Several of these homes were made from bamboo and thatch. Dennis and I enjoy the little ride north. "You know I've heard this place is better than Olongapo" Dennis says as we ride. I thought to myself, "Well that would be something then, to outdo Olongapo?" I would have to see it for myself.

The Jeep nee' stop and we realize we have arrived at Barrio Barretto. The driver gives us a nod to depart, and we see sailors and marines in a now familiar walking the haunch in the P.I. stride, checking inside each bar door for the goodies within.

Dennis and I enter a club for a beer and to our surprise it's packed with sailors and marines seated around a bar corral, zinging coins at stacks of pesos balanced upon the top of a beer bottle within the corral. Glass shatters as the pesos strike the empty beer bottles. The patrons cheer as the glass is swept up and another bottle is dutifully lined up by the bar girls and the throwing of the pesos continues. The DJ breaks the silence as the dancers prepare for the show. A show I wondered, what kind of show. Contortionists and other odd acts take the stage. The beer bottle trick performed by one dancer is as you can imagine. She takes the large end and inserts. Stretching wide and squirming around for all to get a good look. I couldn't believe what I was seeing. The thought of the bottle breaking was on everyone's mind. This same dancer picking up tips of pesos from the floor didn't stop there. She stacks the pesos atop a bottle and makes change as well. What kind of tricks are these I thought. This was really something out of my realm of civilized thinking. The main event the dancer reaches into a large round covered basket she extracts a little yellow baby chicken. Tweeting and squeaking, I thought no way...

The dancer walks around the corral of the bar in the midst of pop eyed squids and jar-heads and does the unthinkable. In goes the baby chick for a warm and wet nest. Dennis and I look around the room and like everyone else are completely aghast at the thought of what the baby chick is going through. The dancer walks around the corral as if nothing was out of the norm. The pesos were thrown into the corral with fervor as drunken sailors and marines could only appreciate the show. Laughter and cheering reach a crescendo, the dancer drawing a sense of accomplishment from the feat. Once the dancer surmised the tips were exhausted and the pesos began to slow, rising from the floor directly on the bar in front of me and Dennis. She stomps her foot a few times and flops out onto the bar, with dampened little wings the baby chick writhes as the nerves continue to flip and flop. The Philippines are proving to be something my little mind was not prepared for.

With our initial thirst for a cold one satisfied, Dennis and I leave the baby chicken show and spend the day exploring the Barrio, bar to bar and club to club drinking a beer at each door and changing women faster than a pair of socks. This fantasyland becomes reality, as we step into yet another shocker of a club called the Flamingo. Adorned walls with Marine Corps flags and other jarhead memorabilia, several of the grunts sitting at the tables it is evident we have entered a Marine hang out. We enter this dusty little joint with a clanky jukebox in the corner spitting out Highway Star by Deep Purple,

Dennis and I saunter in and take a pool table in the corner. Racking up the balls Dennis takes the first shot, "Crack!" the pool balls break as a few marines come over to watch. One marine private calling for a marine vs. sailor challenge on the pool tables Dennis and I accept. Game after game the Bostonian Dennis beats the jar heads at their own game and Dennis wins a round of beer with each win. The marines pony up their beer rounds with a grudging reluctance, a little pissed off that these sailors are taking their turf. The novelty soon wears off and Dennis and I thank the grunts for the brew and begin to leave. One of the marines, "Hey let's make another bet. Come on over here" Dennis and I are reluctant, "Come on give us a chance to win a beer or two" the marine pleads. We agree and sit at a large round table, "What do you have in mind?" Dennis asks.

"Have you ever played SMILES" the jarhead asked. "No, what's "smiles?" Dennis replied. "Well two guys sit at a table and two girls get under the table, the girls perform, well let's just say they perform and the first to come up from under the table and smile, well that guy loses. Are you game?" Dennis accepts and I'm not too sure he'll win. "Dennis we've been at sea for a while and these marines are stationed here." I said. "In the bag Charlie" Dennis confidently replies. The bet is on and Dennis sits back in his chair. I and the others leave the table stand and watch the contest, table bumping and chairs' scooting, only the girls knees can be seen kneeling under the table. Within a few minutes Dennis begins to contort and face grimacing trying to hold on...just as I figured. His girl arises from under the table first with a big smile. Dennis composing himself calls the waitress for another round for the bar. The Marines applaud and pat their comrade on the back. Dennis red faced and defeated, plops a hundred peso bill onto the table.

It was after this that Dennis and I decided before making any more bets we should get better acquainted with all the customs in the clubs before losing any more money. It would be almost impossible to visit them all but we were going to try.

Chapter 7

THE CLUBS

From Olongapo to Barrio Baretto, our private little playground held many surprises. The clubs, the people, the exotic and unfamiliar culture was a lot to digest. Not to mention the little barbeque grill monkey meat. Devil's Den, the Nipa Hut, Midnight Rambler, and Valley of the Dolls are the standouts from the regular naked dancing girls and cold beer. These clubs offered something unique.

Devil's Den – a little hole in the wall with two large rooms one for playing pool and the other for girls. Not so weird huh? Not until you go out back. Behind this club is a pit around 15 feet deep and 20 feet wide. Dirty green water at the bottom was home to an 8 foot crocodile. A sad representation of the majestic creature has existed at the bottom of this hole for who knows how long. However the croc was well fed. Out of a small kiosk was an old man selling baby chicks 3 for a 20 pesos or one dollar. Sailors and Marines would purchase the crocs food for the day from the old man. At the bottom of this pit some chicks still survived the croc and huddled in the corner. Other chicks were dead inside the pit. The croc had cigarette burns on its hide from frustrated customers trying to provoke the animal into consuming the baby chicks on a full stomach.

Midnight Rambler – Another little dive in Barrio Barretto this bar featured several girls dressed in different outfits, a jukebox and pool tables and foosball tables, again seemingly plain. However just outside the back entrance was a tree. On that tree was a platform, home to a large monkey. This monkey was tied to the tree with a leash. Still not so unusual until you saw the pile of empty San Miguel bottles at the bottom of the tree. The monkey, nicknamed San Miguel, had become a true alcoholic. Drunken sailors would challenge the monkey to a chugging contest. Tipping the bottle with its foot and opposable thumb the beer bellied monkey looked as if it was ready to pop. Chugging away, the monkey would beat sailor after sailor as it sucked down each and every drop of the beer, dropping the bottle in the pile at the bottom of the tree. Each group of sailors pony up their cash for each bet lost to the monkey.

Valley of the Dolls – A brightly painted exterior concrete block building the Valley of the Dolls is home to hundreds of brightly body painted dancers with absolutely nothing on but body paint and glitter. At least a six to one ratio, dancers to patrons, the Valley of the Dolls was a clearinghouse of flesh. All types of women have long hair, short hair, big breasts or small ones. Long legs, nice butt, smile, eyes you name it seemed to be a toy box of women for you to choose which one to play with for the evening. For a 19 year old sailor that's been out to sea for several weeks this was the candy shop.

The Nipa Hut – A bamboo walled and thatched roof combination of huts on big wooden plank platforms this was the most unusual bar I had ever visited in the Philippines. Located in Angeles City, just an hour from Subic this club housed every manner of perversion that could be dreamt up in a stage show. Dozens of girls gyrate their bare vaginas in your face, singing a song to eat it all in unison. The stage show opens. With flasks of bamboo cups filled with "Gorilla Juice", a grape flavored concoction of several different rums, and Nipa Hut head bands wrapped around our heads, we all settled in for the shock of our lives. The pet show was a cat caged in a narrow cage with an opening at the end. A trained monkey comes down from a perch and has intercourse with the cat. The cat, stiff as a board, indulges the monkey until the inevitable result and the monkey is then rewarded with a standard treat and taken back to the perch. A stage blow job for a willing volunteer takes place soon after. One drunken sailor with his parts for all to see is given compliments of the house from a stage performer. The last act was a free round of drinks given to the lucky sailor that had an appetite, an appetite for a cooked hot dog. This hot dog wasn't cooked in the normal way that you would think. A stage performer inserts the dog in that particular oven that is moist and steamy inside and walks around the stage surrounded by bar seating. A game show song is playing from the DJ and like musical chairs the stage performer ejects the hot dog onto the chest of one individual seated at the bar. If he eats it, he and his friends get a free round of Gorilla Juice. Ironically, like football players scrambling for a fumbled football, half a dozen drunken sailors scramble for the hot dog to be the first one to take a bite.

Xanadu Club – This club was located just off the bridge in Subic. Large neon strobe lights on the outside lit up the entire corner. Inside dark but lit with only black lighting giving the bikinis a fluorescent glow. Several levels of dance floors with go-go dancers in cages on every level you could only see the costumes move. Each booth could seat 10 people and hold several beers in the middle in a sunken chest of ice. The DJ booth pounded out 80's dance music, as the go-go dancers filled the stages and cages with serpentine dance moves and seductive eye contact.

The White Rock Hotel – This hotel was the closest thing to luxury accommodations that Barrio Baretto could muster up. It had a modern lobby with marble floors and good rooms with central heating and a/c. Hot water too. This wasn't a night club but was a gathering place of several scantily clad bar girls to come and enjoy the swimming pool during the day. The swimming pool had several stone perches in the center on which the half naked beauties could sunbathe. Finding the pool a convenient place to meet servicemen, the sunny pool perches at the White Rock offered the only scenery better than the open sea.

Magsaysay Café – This isn't a night club but an open air café on the Olongapo strip. Several tables arranged sidewalk café style along the boulevard that serves fast food and of course beer. This café is unique because of the wide array of freaks that stop in and eat. The freaks consist of stage performers still in costume, people with oddities, and street vendors that perform magic tricks, bar tricks or other unusual talent.

Taking our party in the early morning around 1 a.m. my friends and I had a late night munch craving, that hunger that arrives in the wee morning hours after a hard night of partying. We stopped into Magsaysay café since no Taco Bell was available, and decided this was the place to munch. After checking our pockets a little low on funds we decided to buy our midnight munch from a passing street vendor. A skinny little wrinkled man passing by with a bamboo pole draped across his shoulders with a bucket on each end. Within the buckets were clutches of boiled eggs - balut. Ballut, a chicken egg with a partially developed embryo that is hard boiled. Once the shell is peeled back, the consumer can then see the embryo curled into a fetal position with little blue eyelids and a vein purple and yellow yolk sack that is transitioning into the embryos organs. Tiny featherless wings, and sometimes with a few feathers, little knobby and knuckled feet are folded along its little body and the beak with its little nostril and facial features clearly visible and developed.

Peeling back the damp shell, the horror of my life appeared before me. This little ball of gooey hell, the facial expression of the little embryo seems to smile as this was its' final revenge, to sicken the stomach of that person that is about to consume it. With a queasy stomach we all decided to eat one together, a shared nightmare that we were all going to live. Gazing upon this little delicacy it was one, two, three, and took a bite into the ballut halfway into the egg. As I am chewing the texture is the consistency of a mix of little crunchy bones and gushy jelly. My tongue swirls around this crunchy mud between chews, and then down the gullet into a growling beer vat of a stomach.

Jonnie begins to chirp and gurgle as he chokes down the ballut. Taking a quick swig of his ice cold San Miguel he keeps the Filipino fast food down. We all struggle with the first bites but as we become accustomed to the new experience we begin to eat more. The little old man drops his pole and buckets onto the sidewalk as we all randomly choose egg after egg, carefully inspecting each selection for doneness, guessing at the stage of embryo development. "Good ballut huh?" the little man smiles as we all are getting our munching on.

Buckets empty, we all realize that we have polished off two buckets of ballut. That was a serious midnight munch. We pay the polite little man and he collects his empty buckets of egg shells and bamboo pole and heads into anonymousness.

Snuggly tucked into our racks back on the ship we sleep heavy as our bellies are full and pockets are empty. We contemplate the next day's events.

It's a little late in the morning and the coffee is a bit over brewed and black. Tank Juice as it is referred. My friends and I, refreshed with hot showers and coffee from the divisional office, have crawled out of our metal coffins and are ready for the day. We share our stories of the night before with the skeleton crew managing the shop and are anxious to get back out there. Filling out pockets with more pesos we head for the quarterdeck to depart for our next adventure. Emerging from the berthing compartment and onto the weather decks the day is hot and the smell of Shit River fills the air. "Let's get away from this stinking river", Don said. We all agree to head up to Barrio Baretto. A half hour and another jeep nee ride later we find ourselves in the Barrio. Pothole ridden streets and little roads scrawl along a narrow boulevard with small shops and of course little holes in the wall bars. Some of the side roads are not even paved and grass huts are in the hills.

Finding our way to a two story balcony bar we settle in order our beers and begin to play some pool. The girls, ever present, walk around the balcony floor completely topless. The sun, the heat, they felt comfort over-trumped modesty. Of course we could have complained to the management but who would listen. After several hours of drinking, the trips to the head were frequent.

A urinal trough with a small copper tube runs the length of the trough, hanging over the basin it dribbles water to keep it flushed. Standing at the trough with my friend Jose' the full bladder is taking its' time to empty. Mine must be a little fuller as Jose' finishes. Suddenly Jose', drunk as a skunk, leans down and dips his head under the copper tube dripping water. He slurps and takes a sip. "Dude what are you doing?" I yell. He stands up and with a drunken smile, "What?" "Dude you just drank from the toilet!" I said. "Were you that thirsty?" I couldn't stop laughing. Jose wipes his chin with a look of pure satisfaction that his thirst was quenched, shakes off the realization of what he's just done. Taking this back to my friends, they all laugh at Jose' and order him another beer. With our feet propped up on the railing of the balcony overlooking the parking lot we view the goings on around the barrio. Whistling at the dancers headed for the clubs. Inevitably a young kid maybe 12 or 13 years old happens by the balcony and says, "Peso Mister?" holding his hand up to the group. Scrambling through our pockets we toss down a couple of penny coins and other little coins, who knows of what value, go over the rail as well. There, we've done our good deed for the day. Other youngsters happen by and see that this little request for coins worked so they tried us as well. "Peso, Peso!" We tossed a few more coins. In a short while a small crowd had gathered below "Peso, Peso!" and we continued to toss over coins. Running out of change we yell back to the bar girls, "Bring us more change", the bartender handing a topless honey several coins for a few 20 peso bills. The bartender emptied her coin box of every sort of coin she had. Pockets now bulging with little coins of all sorts we began to appease the hungry calls of the people below. Drunk we continue to be amused by the spectacle. A call from the left side "Peso, Peso!", and three or four coins were tossed to the left, the crowd would surge to the left. Like a stampede trampling all those in the front, tossing three or four coins to the right, and again the crowd surges stampeding everything in the front. We drop a 5 peso bill, fluttering down like a leaf falling from a tree several hands desperately grasp the air grabbing for the bill. Laughing at the spectacle of the mindless mob we eventually realize that this is not the good deed we had intended. Instead of feeding a few hungry people we had managed to create a mindless mob willing to stomp the hands of those grabbing for the coins. Sadly we had to consider the safety of our approach to feeding the hungry and discontinue appeasing the beggars. The reality of their suffering became evident as it was poverty beyond what I had ever experienced in my childhood. I stopped throwing the coins. It was at this moment I realized a change of port would probably do us all some good. We were becoming numb to our environment.

Chapter 8

A COLD KOREA

The ship is resupplied and the Constellation and her escorts have long since left Subic. The Proteus has remained in Subic for nearly a month and now it is time to leave for another few weeks at sea and to another working port.

Back into sailor mode we gather our thoughts of a liberty port that had proven more than anyone's expectations. The stories from the vets at the steel beach picnic had proven true. The crew worked hard and played even harder. We readied the ship to leave the lights of Subic behind. Off into the South China Sea, the mooring lines to the ship were pulled in. The rolling balance of our sea legs was again being tested as the sea deepened and the waves turned to a deep royal blue. The crew settled into its regular routine of shift work, three meals a day, drills, standing watch and training sessions. Stale rerun movies again were being played in regular schedules on the closed circuit television system and letters were again being written by those lonely sailors in the crew's lounge. The laughter of sailors can be heard over card games at tables with ash trays full to the brim with butts and empty "gedunk" (candy) wrappers. The "Pig" was again alive with her crew.

Chinhae, South Korea was our destination and we wondered if nothing could top Subic but we were all up for the experience and a change of scenery. The sea was choppy and the weather was turning cold. The Philippines are a tropical environment and as we sail north our pea coats become essential uniforms for the biting cold sea air. The old Proteus was handling the choppy sea conditions well as we steamed into the South China Sea.

It was time for open bridge watch, a telephone talker for the officer of the deck, repeating his commands to the steering and combat information center to navigate the ship. Plotting the courses for the ship and notating his commands on a grease pencil board. This watch was strenuous, alertness and higher than average wits were required for this job. I had the eight o'clock p.m. to twelve o'clock a.m. watch and was relieved at that time. During this watch the sea water became colder and the wind began to pick up. An icy wind chill of 12 degrees cut right through you. Exposed to the elements, little bright flakes begin to sprinkle down in the darkness, upon all the watch standers in the open bridge. We grimaced with cold and soon the snow became a sleeting sheet of ice flakes and frozen rain. The ship hit the waves hard as it bobbed up one large wave and down onto the next. The sea spray from the impact would spray a fine mist onto the open bridge watch standers. Frozen crystals began to accumulate on our pea coats, ski caps and equipment. My fingers were cold and difficult to move to write with the grease pencil. It became hard to speak into the sound powered telephone mouthpiece as my lips were purple numb. My mind thought back to those sunny balconies in Barrio Barretto or even the picnic tables back at Barney's at the Beach on Guam. I just wanted warmth.

The midnight hour approaches and we've been splashed with frozen sea spray and rain for nearly three and half hours. I'm so ready to be relieved. My mind is on the midnight ration meal, a meal of galley leftovers from the previous few days' meals. The mid-rats were heated up by the night cook and fed to the late watches to prevent wasted food and free up space in the galley. My knit cap is frozen and ice has accumulated on my eyebrows, and finally I see my relief walking up the ice accumulated steps to the open bridge. Clinging to the icicle railings of the ladder my relief is refreshed and dry.

I give the relief watch my telephone set and grease pencil and request the officer of the deck to be relieved and it is granted. Making my way to the mess decks, I struggle with the outdoor hatch to the passageway as the door is frozen shut. Finally the ice cracks and the hatch opens and I enter the warmth of the interior of the ship. The bright lights of the mess decks appear through the dark corridors and I can smell the mid-rats and hot coffee.

Other late watch standers begin to accumulate on the mess decks for their late meal. My hands thaw against the warmth of the coffee urn and the feeling in my lips begins to come back. Once the movement comes back to my blue lips, I place my tray on the stainless steel counter top of the buffet line. The late cook looks at me as if I am a freak. Frozen eyebrows and peacoat I point to the black hamburger steaks, the cook asks, "How cold is it out there?" I can't believe that it isn't obvious. "Very cold" Is all my mouth could move with an answer, "How about a couple of those hockey pucks there with rice and a slather of the baby poop gravy". The mess cook slops the warmed up feast onto my tray. Hardened hamburger patties with melted cheese, half crunchy rice, runny gravy and green beans with a hot cup of tank juice. Sitting down in the mess deck bucket seats I never thought I could enjoy warmed up leftovers so much losing myself in the meal. I barely take notice of the puddle of melted sea water accumulating in the seat. I began to question myself in my frozen agony why I joined, for this? I asked myself and then I remembered the biscuits and gravy that my mom served the recruiter at my house when I signed the paperwork to join. These little leftovers brought my mind back to home and gave me comfort, I finally appreciated the modest meals back home.

Finding my way back to berthing, fumbling around in the dark, I remove my wet clothes and settle into my rack for the night. I ignored the snoring of 30 other men as my head hit the pillow. I was never so tired. Chinhae was only a day away and I looked forward to no more frozen open bridge watches for a while.

Chinhae, Korea is the coldest place on earth. We man the rails for a fair weather parade, a show of strength when an American ship enters a foreign harbor. The crew dresses in dress uniforms and lines the railings of the ship called fair weather parade and enters the bay outside of Chinhae. As though the cruel thought of standing in the freezing cold in dress uniforms wasn't bad enough, the ship anchored out in the harbor a mile from the pier in heavy fog. No one saw the fair weather parade.

Taking our fairweather parade back to the divisional shop we all transition back into our dungarees. Being a submarine tender two submarines pop up next to the ship, Los Angeles class fast attacks. Our crane booms extend as the work on the submarines commence. Korea, definitely still considered a war zone, and we were here to support the Team Spirit Military Games. Team Spirit annual mock military games that all allied countries of the Pacific participated in case of attack from North Korea. Naval forces from Italy, South Korea, United States and Australia just to name a few, participated. I was curious to meet some of our allies and to see what Korea had in store.

After the eve shift, liberty was again granted and a line formed on the weather deck to a narrow ladder leading to the water. Since being anchored out in the bay we had to shuttle to the pier on flat bottomed boats to go on liberty. Ships launches were shuttling back and forth to the pier. Boatswain-mates were shouting commands and maneuvering the launches, flat bottomed troop carriers, to the narrow ladder. The diesel smoke from the boat engines belches into the thin cold air. Climbing down the ladders our little group made it to the launch. Cold conditions, wind and splash of seawater made the liberty launch a cold and misty ride.

Once on shore there was a base with all of the base necessities, a Laundromat, cantina, an enlisted men's club, Base Exchange. Of course I wasn't interested in seeing historical sites or photographing the mysterious culture, where the action was. We walked through the little base and on to the enlisted men's club. As we walked I noticed a little shop with steam coming from pipes that protruded from the rooftop. A little barber shop sign was out front and I contemplated getting a haircut. Our regular group of friends entered the enlisted men's club and ordered the Korean national beer OB. OB beer has been brewed in Korea since the 1970's and has held its own against other popular brands, so while in Korea do as the Roman's. Sipping our beer and enjoying the break from being at sea we settle into our bar stools, when in walks another shipmate from the ADP department Petty Officer Zimble. We notice Zimble's hair is wet and his face has a glow about it. We ask, "So Zimble what's the story with the wet hair?" Zimble replies, "Well didn't you guys know there is a massage parlor next door?" Surprised that we could get a hot massage and face wrap next door, I realized what the little barbershop sign and steamy pipes were. I was sold.

"Hey you guys I've got a little kink here in my neck, I think I'm going for one of those massages". Jonnie shaking his head, "We'll be here when you're finished"

Sipping the last slug from my pilsner glass of OB, I took leave of our group and headed next door to a little building with a barbershop sign out front. Within the entrance to the parlor two separate rooms, one on the right and one on the left. The steamy warmth of the hot tubs thaws me as I enter. There were a couple of servicemen waiting on the bench outside the door on the right and none on the left. So thinking of my friends back at the enlisted men's club that are patiently waiting, I took the door on the left and knocked. The door opens and out pops a silken haired Korean beauty in a tiny red one piece bathing suit. Her warm smile and perky boobies greet you, "You can put your coat over there" pointing to coat pins on the wall. "Go ahead inside and wait". Her English was not bad. I felt for the other servicemen still sitting on the benches outside the first door. I thought my luck was with me today. I enter the room, "take off those clothes, shower off and get in the tub, it'll just be a minute", she said gently closing the door behind her as it quietly clicks shut. The room has a two person Jacuzzi tub steaming and bubbling.

The bubbling pop and splash of the warm water sounds inviting and I can't wait to get in. The temperature gauge reads 110 degrees. Slowly I place one foot over the edge and my body adjusts to the temperature. I settle into the tub and melt.

Oh yes, ah, I was looking forward to this I thought. It's been a long cold cruise to this place. Melting into the tub I enjoy the hot soak. I observe a massage table next to the wall complete with a paper lining. A shower stall in the corner and several towels neatly folded sit in stacks on a wall shelf. A small end table sits next to the wall with all sorts of creams, gels and lubricants. I wondered when my little honey would come back and I could get a massage. I lay my head back and place a hot towel upon my face and begin to relax when the click of the door turns and she walks. "You ready?" she asks. The voice seems different to me. English was broken. I wondered who was in the room. Rising slightly from my relaxed state, I remove the towel and to my sheer surprise a curly haired beast of a woman with buck teeth, arms and shoulders as big as an Olympic wrestler dressed in cotton warm up pants and a green t-shirt begins to prepare the massage table with towels and pillows. "Where's the other girl?" I ask. In broken English, "Oh she over there", she replies, pointing to the first room, the room on the right with the full bench. Those bastards, I thought, they didn't even warn me. Luck was not with me this day. As fate would have it, in the position I find myself in, I'm at the mercy of the Korean wrestler woman. She towels me down from the steamy water of the hot tub and shows me to the massage table, smiling with her crooked smile and one slightly crossed eye. Climbing upon the massage table I sympathetically accept her services. Surprisingly, I enjoy her technique as the strength in her hands kneaded my sore muscles like pizza dough. "You like?" she asks. "Yes, yes of course… good job." I reply hoping the experience will be finished quickly. Finishing my back massage thoroughly she turns me over onto my back and her hands find her way beneath my waist "I do a good job here too, you give me a tip?" I think for a moment, why the hell not. She lubricates her hands with those creams on the end table and begins to massage. I close my eyes and try to imagine the other girl, the one that greeted me when I entered. Surprisingly the wrestling girl's technique is quite good, I'm enjoying it. Trying hard to use my imagination, I just couldn't get to that magic moment when I would have the inevitable relief. The girl, "let me do this" as she takes off the green t-shirt. Lopsided and sagging bags of fish oil with long nipples didn't make the ordeal any easier. Finally, she pulled the bunny out of the hat and her tip was well earned. I shower, get dressed and begin to return to my friends in the enlisted men's club. Leaving the steamy little hallway into the open air I walked through the parking lot and back to the enlisted men's club. Disgusted with myself and what I've just endured I contemplate what the hell I'm going to say to my friends. Maybe they'll forget. Maybe they won't ask. Not a chance.

Once back with my friends the very first thing they ask is how was the experience. I remained coy and evasive but Jonnie realizes I'm hiding something. He knows me well by now, "Come on Charlie, how was it?" he presses on. Trying to save face, I rave about how relaxing it was to get a massage with a great tug job to boot, conveniently leaving out the appearance of my hostess. I describe the hand technique, the gels, creams and the warmth of the hot tub. They eagerly listen and are contemplating their own massage and I believe they are sold on my experience. Jonnie seems to be sipping his beer a little faster and seems anxious to finish up. "Yeah, I think I'll go get a massage tomorrow," he says. "Do you recommend a masseuse?" he asks. As if an evil angel suggests something in my ear, I then recommend he takes the room on the left as they enter the parlor, you know the one with the empty bench.

After having another beer, my friends and I exchange our money for the Korean Wan and head off base to

explore the town of Chinhae, South Korea. It was early
March and the cherry blossoms were in bloom despite
the cold chill in the air. The Koreans were celebrating
the Cherry Blossom Festival. The town was decorated
and festive. Several vendor stands with tiny strings of
Christmas lights and tents lined the streets, filled with
homemade wooden furniture, seashell decorations,
jewelry, dried goods, eel skin wallets and purses, fake
mink blankets, coats, shoes, even food stands selling
steaming hot soup and noodles. I and my friends visit
the little stands looking at all the items, trying to figure
out what some of the food is. A flattened fish that has
a facial expression of a demon called a devil fish hangs
from strings on one of the stands. The most grotesque
thing I've seen so far on the cruise. The expression on
the fish appears as though it is in agony. Large red sea
urchins with sharp red barbs hang from another stand,
oozing some sort of slime. Dried eel jerky strips, fish of
all sorts and Asian pears fill wooden boxes on farmer's
market tables. Korean women dutifully sweep their areas
with small hand held straw brooms. And after several
hours of walking and pondering over the local goods, our
amusement slowly gives way to hunger, and we decide to
get something to eat.

Walking along the streets of Chinhae the foreign
signs are all in Korean and we cannot read which one

may be someplace to eat. We see a sign with a painted bowl and steam rising from it, and determine this may be a place to eat. We enter the door and climb a small stairway into a balcony setting indoors. A small cast iron stove burns lumps of coal in the corner, the only source of heat. An older woman dressed in a stitched silk dress with ornate floral designs greets us. Surprised to see several Americans within her establishment she directs us to remove our coats and shoes pointing to silk pillows around a long table. We all remove our shoes and sit, legs crossed on these small flat pillows on the floor, surrounding this rectangular table. Tea is politely served along with little bowls of soup as a first course. The Korean host has a delicate and motherly demeanor. Then the main course, large chicken fried steaks with fresh vegetables and rice with a yellow gravy. This seemed like a very traditional meal for us, nothing unusual to the American pallet. We stuff our gobs with the home cooked meal as our hostess patiently tends to our every need. We have all longed for a lovingly home cooked meal, and other than being a Korean woman, she reminds me of how my mother cooks back home. She seems to enjoy that the Americans are eating her cooking and delights in our satisfaction. We thank the nice hostess with several Won in tips.

Having eaten our fill the sailor in us has the curious thought of getting a beer. We have heard that there is one place here in Chinhae that serves Americans "Donna's Greenhouse Pub" The Greenhouse, the only pub that really was an American hangout in Chinhae was a shell of a building. Cold and uninviting inside were unpainted concrete block walls with little décor, wobbly round tables with regular cafeteria chairs and a well worn bar, served all the regular Asian beers, Japanese, Korean and Filipino San Miguel. Also champagne called "Oscar". Oscar comes in two flavors, peach and grape that were bottled in a typical green wine bottle with a gold label and twist off cap. Several hostess girls worked the pub and kept the lonely sailors company. My friends and I enter and take a seat at one of the wobbly tables with the uneven legs and order. Remembering the peach schnapps "Brain Hemorrhages" experience from Uncle Bobs back on Guam, I ordered up a bottle of the grape Oscar. Screwing off the cap, I poured a healthy glass of the grape Korean champagne for myself and took a sip. "How is it?" Don asked. "Not bad. Do you want a glass" I asked Don. "No I'll stick with this" being a devout beer drinker he picks up his brew and tipping it towards me, takes a slug. I tip my glass and drink down the glass of Oscar. It's very sweet and is almost like drinking grape soda pop except with a wine quality. This stuff is going down easy. Some of the other guys take a small sip and kind of appreciate the difference in the experience but still stick with their beers. I'm the only one ordering up more bottles of the sweet champagne. Glass after glass of Oscar I'm enjoying a light buzz beginning to take over my senses. Into my third bottle, and buzzing pretty good by now, I'm asking every female Korean go-go dancer in the place to dance. Finally I scored. A finely curved Korean girl reluctantly takes my sloppy ass to the dance floor. She is polite and smiles as we begin to bump and grind like little monkeys. After a song or two, I look over at my friends laughing their asses off. Realizing my movements are short and choppy, my mind becomes blurred ooze. My joints become like an erector set that has been screwed too tightly and my back is as stiff as a board. My dancing looks like the tin man without the oil. I continue to try and dance with the girl, realizing I'm stumbling and nearly fall. The dance floor appears like sea water and my sea legs are failing to keep me balanced. Focusing on my balance and regaining my composure, I have realized the polite Korean girl has left me to my own embarrassment, I return to the table of my friends. Congratulating me on making a complete fool of myself, Jonnie yells, "Hey Charlie, do you know what this stuff is?" as he holds up an empty bottle of Oscar pointing to the back label. "What the hell is this shit?" I look at the two bottles he's holding up or is it just one, I can't tell. "It's opium based," he says. "What?" I reply. Hollering over the music Jonnie again, "It has opium in it. It will get you racked bad." Whether or not this was accurate I had not felt a drunken buzz like this ever before that was for sure. I couldn't begin to contemplate on how I was going to maintain for the rest of the night. The evening was still young and I'm already waxed. After sitting down and getting my breath and balance my head is still swimming. People's faces become contorted like silly putty and their words become slow. The concrete block walls appear as if they are fluid and pulse and swell back and forth. As if in a surreal dream, I see other Proteus sailors laughing at their table smiles and grins stretch along the outermost corners of their faces. Talking amongst each other, their voices echo in my mind. I convince Dennis from Boston to leave the Greenhouse with me and take me back to the ship. Walking back to the ship's launches that night was a challenge. It would seem like I was walking fast but I wasn't. I was walking slowly. What seemed like walking 100 feet or so really wasn't, it really was about 20 feet. I had a hard time speaking and judging distance as my body seemed to work harder to move. My joints and legs were stiff and must have looked like a wandering mummy. The only benefit to how I was feeling is that

I didn't notice the cold. I had sufficiently numbed my body to not feel the sting of the cold air.

Arriving at the pier, several sailors are there waiting for the launch to arrive. The twinkling lights of the ship in the distance mesmerized me. I took leave of the group and walked a small distance to a little spot down the concrete parking lot behind a trash dumpster. I had to pee. Into the water seemed the logical choice in which to pee so down into the bay water it went. To my surprise the water began to glow neon green around the disturbance in the water. I thought I was seeing things. Was this the Oscar fucking with my head, I couldn't tell. I thought the sooner I was onboard the ship the happier I will be. Returning to the group, they laugh again when I explain what just happened. They explain that it's normal, that there are small organisms within the sea water that glow green when disturbed and that I'm not going crazy. Late the next morning I'm getting ready for my shift. Jonnie, "So how are ya' feelin' this morning Charlie?" grinning from ear to ear. He knew that I was feeling pretty hard. "Never again" I replied. I pledged I would never touch another bottle of Oscar again. Laughing at my misfortune, Jonnie prepares to go on liberty. "So what are you up to?" I ask. "Going to go get that massage right now" he replies. Knowing what he is in for, nodding and smiling I quietly get the last laugh.

After another couple of days' onboard working shift and writing a few letters was a brief respite from the partying. It was time to see more of that exotic culture of Korea. Certainly, a tug job, the cherry blossom festival and a few bottles of Oscar were not all Korea had to offer. No, my friends and I didn't grab cameras to photograph ancient Buddhist temples or spend our money in the many shopping districts where goods are manufactured and sold at a fraction of the cost you would pay in an American mall, or even exploring the rich culture of the Korean people. We didn't explore the base or meet other people stationed there at the enlisted men's club. No, it was off to Texas Street in Busan, an entertainment district 30 minutes north of Chinhae that catered to the Team Spirit fleets. Korean brothels, booze and boobs galore, flashy lights, loud music pumped through large speakers in row upon row of bars was our destination.

A cab ride around mountainous curves in the Korean countryside is the established route of the local cabbies familiar with the typical sailor requests. The cab driver hits each curve with too much speed barely staying off the guard rails. Deep gorges of sloped rice paddy covered hills and small villages on the way until Pusan are visibly evident, we would yell at each twist and turn our driver barely missing the edge. Our fear of falling over the craggy rice patty hills would bring a grin to the reckless

Korean taxi driver. Pusan, a large Korean town with busy traffic we tell the cabby, "Texas Street?" He seems to have heard this before as he hasn't spoken a word of English but still manages to get us to our destination.

Piling out of the cab, we tip the driver and he asks "Good ride for you?" smiles and disappears to the next call. We find ourselves again in an amusement park of bars and flashy lights. Sailors from several countries and ROK (Republic of Korea) marines walk the boulevards. Obviously here for team spirit, they are all enjoying the sights and sounds. We are no exception. "This one here seems to be as good as any" Don said. So we all enter. Once inside and take a seat, Timbo, Jonnie, Don and Dave sit at a round table. Enjoying the music from a large brightly lit jukebox and go-go girls in lingerie, we see the most incredible sight, a black see through teddy with lace panties walking towards us, the largest natural Asian knockers I have ever seen, rugby footballs with the bounce and jiggle of Jell-O. Holy shit! Dave exclaimed. Arriving at our table the Korean comfort girl asks to sit down, "Buy me drinky?" Seeing the natural beauties under that teddy that arrived before she did, Dave without hesitation reaches into his pocket, "Hell yeah Honey." During the next few hours Dave and I take turns buying drinks for the busty Korean comfort girl, motor-boating our faces into the softest Asian pillows in West Pac history.

Several sailors from the team spirit exercises occupy every corner of the lingerie club, Australians, Italians, Koreans and Americans all shelling out plenty of Won for the booze and bar girls. They share their stories of the Team Spirit exercises and enjoy the company of the multi-national atmosphere.

Timbo takes out some coins and heads to the old jukebox that just ran out of songs. "Anything special?" he asks. "Just the usual" Don replied. The usual being rock and roll. As Timbo clicks away the selections on the jukebox, boisterous singing erupts from a group of Italian sailors into national songs of pride. Loud and boisterous they take advantage of the silent jukebox for a moment, all arm-in-arm swaying to the hefty heaving of beer mugs. In reply Australians begin their Yo-ho-ho songs of the sea, again loud and full of national pride they sing their nationalistic best. Looking around at the other Americans within the bar we struggle to find a song we all know. As if bestowed upon us from a guardian angel, the crackle of the jukebox begins to play a song by the rock band Queen, "We are the Champions". Now this is a song we know.

Loudly and full of pride we all raise our beers and sing to our hearts content. Reaching our loudest, "...and we'll keep on fighting 'till the end", at no other moment on this cruise was I so proud to be an American. Here in the middle of team spirit, a foreign nation, amongst several navies, and in a war zone we sang our American pride and no one can do anything about it. Timbo had chosen the right song at the right time. Maybe it was a lucky choice but his resourcefulness came through. Wine women and song, the sailor's motto was certainly in full effect that night.

As the cold days wear on the Proteus remains in Korea for another few weeks a few of us decide to seek a little more culture. Don and I decide to take a train trip to Seoul, the capital of South Korea.

The next day we had a weekend in front of us so Don and I headed for the little train station in Chinhae. A little green train is waiting there boarding passengers for the two hour ride to Seoul. Bustling passengers load their suitcases into the storage compartments as Don and I wait outside the train at a picnic table. Out of the blue a Korean man arrives at our table speaking English. Introducing himself as security he asks to see our identification. Presuming he is an official or police as he was dressed in a long shirt and tie with a picture badge of some sort I present my military i.d. Taking it from my hand the man closes his eyes and seems to be trying to memorize the details of the identification. Thinking this was odd I took my identification card from his hand and asked, "So what did you need that for?" He abruptly rises from the table and quickly walks away. Looking over at Don, we surmise that this country is still in a state of war and that man could have been anyone wanting to see an American military identification card. We agree that we must be more careful going forward.

The bell rings to board and Don and I board the little green train and take a seat amongst all the Korean people. Slowly the wheels begin to squeak and turn down the track.

Pausing briefly at stops to allow more passengers to board, the click clack of the train bumps along the tracks to Seoul. Once at the stops, ROK Marines board, peering from underneath their helmets, they check for any suspicious activity. Randomly they ask passengers for tickets and identification always on the lookout for North Korean infiltrators. Once satisfied, the train is cleared to once again move down the tracks for Seoul. Coming to a stop at the Seoul train station, we get our bags and head for the hotel. Walking the cold streets of Seoul we observe machine gun nests on strategic corners of the city, reinforced with sandbags and concrete. It has become evident to us that Korea is still a very dangerous place, even thirty years after the armistice. It was a reality that again struck me that this country could spiral into chaos and war at any moment. Seoul is also a bustling, busy modern city, a dichotomy against military outposts to say the least.

We settle into a room at the Seoul Hilton, a beautiful tower amongst many high rises and shiny buildings. The room is a suite with silk mattresses that are set on the floors within the rooms. The fridge is stocked with all sorts of little bottles of water, soda and tomato juice. Little liquor bottles in the bar are neatly arranged on the counter. Luxurious compared to my small rack back on the Proteus. Don and I welcome the break from all the debauchery. We roam the shopping districts, restaurants and little rice wine bars. Groups of business men enjoying their company and singing karaoke, drink from the little white cups. We roam the streets some more and are directed by the locals to try out a little burro of Seoul called Itaewon, a sailor's dream, again row upon row of entertainment clubs including dancing girls, stage plays, and booze bars. The lights flash and the sparkle of the glitzy boulevards trap us like insects circling a light bulb. We decide the culture is what we're here for so we take in a Korean concert of singers and other cultural dancing. Don and I were bored to death and couldn't understand the language but appreciated the change in venue. Walking along we stop and see a paper puppet show. Small crowds gather as the paper puppets dance behind shadow paper and dim lights. Don and I appreciate the exotic form of entertainment. After the puppet show we dive into a little drink bar for a beer and are greeted by a ROK Marine, inviting us over to join him into his booth he shouts "Democracy good!" raising his little white cup of sake' he toasts to his new American friends. He buys a round for us and we thank him. He calls over two lovely "company" girls to keep us occupied at the table, his gesture of thanks for his American allies. He orders a table tray of snacks. Not your typical thought of snacks by American standards. Not potato chips, or popcorn, but a round tray with little compartments full of Korean eats. Little sun dried minnows with eyeball and head still attached, dried fish nibbles, olives, sugar coated garlic peanuts, and chewy squid jerky.

We tried our best to communicate with the ROK Marine, to understand his limited English and he was trying to understand our hand gestures and sign language, but as we continued to drink, we all became more and more indiscernible. "Democracy yes!" he would chant as he guzzled large swigs of beer and sake', and we would tip our beers in response. I thought to myself what misery he and his family may have suffered at the hands of the North Koreans. How he was just grateful and happy to have a couple of Americans as company for his evening demonstrated his deepest thanks for helping his country. I reflected on how well our country had it. It made an impression on me that this humble fellow was thankful for his freedom, and what I as an American, even though from poverty, had taken my freedom and the lasting peace in our country for granted.

The night became early morning and it was becoming time to thank our host and get back to the hotel for a good night sleep. We were leaving for Chinhae the next afternoon and still had some cultural shopping to do. We take leave of the girl's company, tip the bar and all head to the sidewalk for a cab back to the hotel, our host chanting "Democracy" the whole way out the door and into the crisp cold air. Outside ROK marines dutifully manning the machine gun emplacements on the street corners endure the cold night air. Speaking in his drunken voice, his breath puffing steam, our new friend shouts in drunken fashion, "Thank you America" as Don and I hail a cab. Entering the cab, we shut the door and rolled down the window, "Thank you again", Don said, saluting as he slammed the cab door shut. The ROK Marine snaps to attention outside the cab door. Standing in the cold air, he salutes back with a big smile and heads down the sidewalk into anonymousness. Again, someone met whose brief encounter was short and memorable.

The next morning we cruise a few markets and spend what little we had left in the pockets on fake mink blankets, shoes and cork carvings and board the little green train back to Chinhae.

Once back in Chinhae the ship was finishing up its mission there and preparing to leave again. I pack the items I bought at the markets in a large box and send them home to my mother back home. I had no room for storage in the berthing space so I had to send those things ahead for when I got back home. And so it was again out to sea saying goodbye to another working port. The crew was tired and fatigued from several days of submarine repairs. So it was on to another port and this time it was just for fun. Hong Kong – Pearl of the Orient.

Chapter 9

HONG KONG – PEARL OF THE ORIENT

After several days at sea and long nights on open bridge watch and equally satisfying sleep, I awaken to bumpy tugboats pushing the Proteus alongside the berth. "Hong Kong" I thought, "We must be here". Stretching my arms and legs I emerge from my tiny rack and the liberty whistle blows. "I've got to get a shower, I'm feeling greasy" I thought. I can taste the "yuck" in my mouth and gather my things to get cleaned up. I get into the showers. No one is here I thought. I notice the ship is like a virtual graveyard. Usually the showers were full and lots of activity in the passageways and compartments, but today was different. I'm thinking as I lather up a good soap, "Plenty of hot water too". I begin to "Hollywood" my shower, taking my time to get all those areas with good hot lathery soap and water. No worries about conserving water or hurrying up and finishing for the next guy. It was just me as the ship was hooked up to pier water, I was in heaven. I appreciate the relief of a good, long, hot shower, no more water hours or conservation hours of water while underway. Pressing my face up into the streams of hot water, it pelts my face and flows into my hair and down my back, "I've got to get out of here" but I just don't want this shower to end. Reluctantly, my wrinkled fingers turn the knobs to the off position, Hong Kong waits.

Opening the hatch to the weather decks, I get my first glimpse of Hong Kong. My eyes adjust to the light and there before me emerges the Pearl of the Orient. Skyscrapers of immense height, shining and glistening in the sun are stacked row upon row into tight compaction. Hong Kong was the queen of cities. I had never seen a city this big before. Buildings of all sorts, office buildings, apartment buildings, and some I don't even know what they are, rising several dozen stories high, I am in awe. They tower above me as giants looking down upon the little Rusty Pig. An urban core modern marvel of construction by millions of Chinese, it is certainly the Pearl of the Orient.

Still a British territory, Hong Kong welcomes the Proteus and other ships of team spirit. I see the Italians, the Australian ship, Greeks and others all with their flags and union jacks flapping in the air, snuggly moored into their berths. Jonnie, Timbo, Don and I take our liberty. Arriving at the fleet landing, a piano lounge and restaurant, we sit at a large table and order our first meal in the new port. White gloved waiters take our orders as wine menus are presented to us. I am certainly out of my element. Having only experienced the lower scale of the economic ladder and trying to take in the experience, I ordered the Peking duck with a glass of white wine. Don and Jonnie order their meals and Timbo some flaming type of dish that is served flambé style at the table. Several sailors from the various fleets are already half way into their meals and drinks. Soldiers from the British garrison stationed on Hong Kong line the large mahogany bar, with the large brass beer taps. The bartender fills their mugs to the brim; they are boisterous and loud, confident in their status within the confines of the fleet club. The Americans have arrived and settled in for the experience. A studious British pianist begins to play "Satin Doll" a classic song of years gone by, on the grand piano in the corner. Tickling the ivories and in grandiose fashion with a deep voice he bellows out the words with a shake of his hair at the high notes and a bow of his chin on the low notes, popping and pounding his hands on the keys. Finishing his song with an air of pompous arrogance he begins to welcome the sailors of the other countries. "Her Royal Highness welcomes her guests to the fleet landing of Hong Kong. Our neighbors Italy and Greece", once he announces the countries the sailors of those countries resound with songs. "Our cousins in the south Australia", again nationalistic songs abound from the Australians. He pauses, "And of course those sailors from (pausing)... the colonies". Laughter arises from the Brits around the mahogany bar mocking the diminutive status of the Americans within their midst. This was the first time in the cruise that I felt insulted and insignificant "Why that arrogant son of a bitch!" I thought.

Sensing a feeling of insult, a small group of sailors from the old Proteus sitting in the corner begin a song, "The Battle of New Orleans' '. "In 1814 we took a little trip, along with Colonel Jackson down the mighty Mississippi. We took a little bacon and we took little beans, and we caught the bloody British in the town of New Orleans. We fired our guns and the British kept a comin' there weren't as many as there was a while ago. We fired once more and they began to runnin', down the Mississippi to the Gulf of Mexico. Yeah they ran through the wires and they ran through the brambles and they ran through the bushes that the rabbit couldn't go. They ran so fast that the hounds couldn't catch 'em down the Mississippi to the Gulf of Mexico". Singing and laughing, the Proteus sailors revel in the lyrics. The look on that pianist face was priceless. A surprised look of how dare you in here. The British soldiers at the bar weren't so jovial anymore and the atmosphere in the place went from fun to ominous. In fact, their faces changed from smiles to grimaces as they began to slowly place their beer mugs down on the bar, they wiped the froth from they're chins. The place begins to quiet as the pianist stops his ramblings, and only the clink of silverware on plates can be heard. An eerie calm begins as the stares across the room from the Brits and Americans becomes thick. You can feel the tension boil, "O.k. gentlemen we're all friends here. Not here, not now", said the pianist as he begins to play an upbeat tune on the ivories, the tension breaks. We all have the impression that it's going to be a long five days in Hong Kong.

After exchanging our money for Hong Kong dollars and paying dinner we roam the streets of the Wanchai district of Hong Kong. Thousands of neon signs written in Chinese hang from open businesses. Brightly lit

tailor shops, exotic restaurants with big boiling vats
of eel and sea urchins. Each of the squiggly creatures
chosen by hungry Chinese patrons from aquariums in
the windows. Artistic and ornate jewelry and crafts,
dragons carved of brilliant green oriental jade and white
elephant tusk ivory, gold necklaces and rings of all sorts,
Asian style rugs and paintings. The shops went on and
on, occasionally dotted with British pubs and tattoo
parlors in their midst. Millions of Chinese went about
their daily tasks, the city was crowded and immense. We
feared that we could get lost quite easily.

Getting a little thirsty, we stop into one of those
little British pubs, "The Horse and Groom". No larger
than a two car garage this tiny hole in the wall was our
refuge. The heavy wooden door opens to a small foyer,
bar with taps of Carlsberg, Guinness and Bass Ale, six
booths along the wall and a small kitchen around the
corner. A menu of the standard British fare was on the
tables. Mince meat pie, roasted chicken or rabbit, and
of course those famous fish and chips. We ordered up a
couple of coldies. A British barmaid pulling the taps was
cordial and asked, "So when did you yanks pull into the
harbor? Come on and sit down, what'll it be for ya?" She
pulls the levers to the taps and pours each beer carefully
and to the brim. "Don't want to short measure ya" she
said, a decent pour of beer if I say so. We take the long

cold sip of the frothy drink, a unanimous sigh of relief from a long afternoon of walking the streets of Wanchai district. Don asks our barmaid, "So honey, what's there to do at night around here?" "Well you have the Makati Inn down the street here" she replies. "It's where our boys go for a little fun". Makati Inn huh...O.k. thanks. "Don't mention it" she replies with a smile. We remember the name of the place and continue with our beers. "Let's go back to the ship and change, we'll check that place out tonight" Don said.

Later that evening my friends and I decked out in our best cities to find the infamous Makati Inn. Sitting with our booth at the Makati Inn, several colored ceiling spot lights, tables surround the dance floor and a DJ booth in the corner. Several women Chinese, British, Filipino all dressed in little miniskirts and fishnet stockings, not bar girls but just regular customers looking for company of the service men smile and strike up conversations with us. A well curved Chinese girl, Gigi and her friends are curious about the Yanks in their midst and take a seat at the table. Asking questions about the states we all share that standard conversation of things back home with our female companions, of course buying them plenty to drink. Gigi and I talk and share each other's company. Her English is quite good.

More British soldiers are at the bar and other tables deep inside the Inn. Other shipmates from the "Pig" already on their second or third round sit at other tables opposite the Brits. The night gets into full swing the Inn becomes packed with wall to wall service men and available women. The dance floor becomes an active pit of gyrating women and American sailors, the Brits seem to be annoyed. Taking exception with a bar full of yanks taking their women and drinking their booze, the British soldiers begin to assert themselves. One in particular seems to be the instigator, pushing his way between the Americans and the girls dancing together on the dance floor. Jealous and full of piss he talks his shit the fed up Yanks on the floor lose their patience. It didn't take much but an insult and a push of a drunken sailor that the allure of fighting an American becomes reality.

When out of the crowd screams arise from frightened girls. The crash of beer glasses on the Makati dance floor becomes a writhing brawl between the Brits and Yanks. Fists begin to fly and glass bottles erupt, chairs, and beer mugs become weapons as the Brits and Yanks go at each other, a chaotic scene of busted knuckles and men being knocked flat with each punch. Slugging and punching the Brits dish out as much as they're taking. The entire bar becomes consumed with Brits and Yanks having it out for rights to the bar. The insults at the Fleet club are remembered this night as the two biggest boys on the block finally remedy those early remarks. The D.J. trying to bring about peace yells into the microphone, "Fighting doesn't solve anything!" The yanks beg to differ, the DJ is ignored and the brawl rages on. Punch after punch the Brits and Yanks have a go at each other, then out of nowhere the club lights come on and the once dark dance floor reveals several Brits and Yanks toe to toe and hand to hand, slugging away. The entire bar is embroiled. The minutes seem like hours as dozens of American Shore Patrol, British MP's and Hong Kong Police suddenly storm into the club and begin breaking up the fight with swinging night sticks. Women and other patrons stand backs flat against the wall as the Brits and Yanks are separated by the crack and thud of the long black night sticks with no real clear winner, the bar closes. "Everyone the bar is now closed" the DJ announces over the microphone. Several sailors and British soldiers lay on the dance floor being placed in plastic handcuffs, others being carried out on stretchers. My friends and I melt into the crowd escaping the bar down the stairs to the sidewalk. Several Hong Kong Police paddy wagons with swirling blue-lights wait for the unlucky participants to emerge for their ride to the brig. Curious crowds of Chinese onlookers stop to get a glimpse of the carnage. Luckily we escape the confusion and head back to the "Horse and Groom".

Flinging open the large wooden door to the Horse and Groom Pub, Timbo, Don, Jonnie and I compose ourselves. Heavy breathing and wide eyed our little group settles in checking ourselves for injuries, we order a couple of pints. In a panic, we begin drinking our jitters off. We can't believe what just happened. All talking about the scuffle at the same time, we barely notice that a bruised and busted British soldier enters. His shirt torn and nose bleeding he begins to take refuge in the little pub. The barmaid yells out "Don't start it here Dickey!" as if she knew the troublemaker. We brace ourselves for another tussle but luckily he sees us sitting there and realizes he is outnumbered turns and leaves. The night passes into the early morning hours as we drink a few well poured pints from the comforting British barmaid. "Don't worry about our boys. They're just looking for some fun." She says.

Back on the Proteus the next day the crew is given a warning that as guests of the Queen we need to behave ourselves in her port, but to stick together if need be. Since Jonnie and Don had duty that day and night clubbing was a dangerous activity, Timbo and I decided to take in a few sights. We had heard about Victoria Peak, the highest peak on Hong Kong Island that overlooks the city into Kowloon, the mainland district across the harbor into China. Grabbing my camera we make our way to the tram stop and get our tickets from a teller window located at the bottom of the peak. The tram itself, a bright red boxcar, can seat 70 people or so in little bench seats with plenty of windows. We both board along with other passengers and the conductor pulls the levers. The turnstiles on the track begin to pull the tram up the steep mountain slope. The safety cables creek and pop under the strain of all the heavy weight of the boxcar full of passengers. Up the steep climb it goes. Timbo and I are nearly lying on our backs as the boxcar climbs the steep slope, reminiscent of the slow climb up the highest track of the Colossus roller coaster at Six Flags in Los Angeles. Ca-chink, Ca-chink, Ca-chink up each rung of the tracks the little tram is pulled, the peak is nearing. Looking back I contemplate the fall if the cable should fail and realize we're at the point of no return. Reaching the top of the peak the little tram squeaks to a stop and Timbo and I climb the remaining stairs to the observation patio. The walk and gardens of Victoria Peak are beautiful. Delicate flowers and plants have been painstakingly manicured and the landscaping is lush. Carefully cleaned sidewalks are dutifully edged. Making our way to the observation deck, we take our first look out over the city. Looking out from the highest vantage point Hong Kong in all its glory is laid out before us. We can see just how vast this city is, hundreds of towers, buildings and even jumbo jets flying into the airport from far- away places disappear behind the jumble of skyscrapers. A wonderful taste of an exotic culture with the flare of modern architecture renewed my sense of this beautiful pearl in all its glory.

As we stand in awe I realize that I have brought my graduation gift, my camera. Timbo teaches me how to use my graduation gift, a new Minolta 35mm camera with zoom lens. He shows me all the attributes and features, as we take several pictures from the view. Snapping away he explains in his methodical way the exposure to light, aperture settings and the different light filters that I can use. It was well worth the trip and the photos came out wonderfully.

Dusk begins to fall upon the city, and I am fortunate enough to have a date with one of the lovely Chinese girls that I met at the Makati. I have to get back to the ship to change to meet Gigi. Long lovely silken black hair, and busty. Unusual for a Chinese girl and coveted by Chinese men, Gigi will accompany me for dinner, drinks and dancing. I've got to meet up at the Fleet Club.

Dressed in a black one piece dancing mini dress and heels, we find our way to the "Horse and Groom". Settling into the large leather booth, she orders the roasted rabbit and me, the fish and chips. We enjoy each others' company with conversation. Sipping her wine she patiently answers my many questions about Hong Kong and her family. I had not really stopped and talked to a woman while on this cruise to get to know them and where the ship was visiting. It was a refreshing change from small talking comfort girls. Sipping down our last bit of wine, and paying the tab, it was time to go dancing. Gigi recommends her favorite club, a famous Hong Kong night spot popular with the Chinese residents of the island, "Suzie Wong's Pussycat Club".

You cannot miss the Pussycat Club. The sign is decorated with hundreds of flashing bulbs in all sorts of colors, red, green, blue and white. The lettering in bright red "Suzie Wong's Pussycat Club" is unmistakable. We enter through the large wooden doors and up a few steps to the main club, several tables, live band and flashy lit dance floor. "This is our favorite place, Chinese girls", she said. I take a look around and see that I and one other shipmate from the Proteus, Seaman Pardo, are the only Americans in the club, the rest of the customers predominantly Chinese. We push our way through the crowd and the heads of the Chinese men turn to see Gigi sauntering through the club with me on her arm. Proud to be seen with an American, she takes my hand and we snuggle into a booth. Gigi crosses those sexy legs with perfectly painted toe nails, the Chinese men continue to stare at her. Finally a perky little Chinese waitress arrives at the table and Gigi orders the drinks in Mandarin Chinese. "Two whisky and cokes", she yells over the thumping music. The waitress nods politely and goes about the task of getting the drinks. The band has an upbeat dance sound that mimics the British band "The Cure", pounding the air with its rhythm. Anticipating the dancing Gigi can't wait to get out on that dance floor. "Let's go dance", she takes my hand again to the dance floor. Bumping, and bouncing Gigi dances to the rhythm. I can feel the stares of the Chinese men on my back. She is a vision to behold.

Arriving back at the table after a few dances, we enjoy our drinks. The drinks go down smooth and easy, as we are thirsty after the dancing. We need to order again. We wait and wait and wait but the waitress doesn't come back. I decided to order from the bar. Politely I excuse myself with a peck on Gigi's cheek, "I'll be right back". I push through the crowd again and arrive at a large wooden bar with brass fixtures. The bartender with his white tuxedo shirt and black pants wipes the bar. "Two whiskey and cokes please" I ask. "No more for you", he replies. "Excuse me?" I said. "No more for you, you go!" he replied. "Hey what's your problem man? I just ordered some drinks and I expect you to serve me.

I'm not drunk!" Just at that moment a push from behind, I knew wasn't the normal bump of a crowded room.

I turn to see a large gorilla of a Chinese bouncer, dressed in a silk suit, with two of his little gargoyle buddies next to him. "You go now!" said the gorilla. "Fuck you asshole! I'm not going anywhere!" I was pissed off and the evening had turned into something I didn't expect. It dawned on me that the jealous Chinese assholes in the club couldn't stand to see an American with a cute Chinese girl. The gorilla and his little buddies begin to swing and the second brawl within two days begins again. Striking their best martial arts stances the fight is on. I plow into the big one first and clock his jaw with everything I've got. The big bouncer falls to the floor and the gargoyles begin to high kick and punch martial arts style. Swinging at one then the other I'm fighting three of the jealous assholes. Two more little bouncers arrive and it's five to one. With my back against the bar, the swinging is frantic. I'm taking three punches to one. I begin to chase one of the little bouncers as he begins to run into a corner. The other continues to punch and kick as my attention turns from the running bouncer back to the main event. Out of nowhere Seaman Pardo, seeing his shipmate getting his ass kicked jumps in. Swinging like a wild man the odds are evening up or so I thought. The Gorilla has now recovered, and seeing

Pardo swinging takes a bottle and breaks it half, stabs Pardo with a jagged edge into his forearm. The band stops playing and pleads for calm.

The crowd encircles the fight as the patrons watch the carnage. I begin to tire and, in desperation, pick up a bar stool and crack it over the head of one of the gargoyles, he falls unconscious to the floor. Pardo bleeding from his arm has a group of three on him, I have four by now, and finally the Gorilla grabs my arms. He and the gargoyles turn me face forward on the bar bending my head over the rail. The bartender, being one with the bouncers, cups a thick glass ashtray in his palm and begins to wallop the crown of my skull. Pop! Pop! Pop! I feel the sting and concussion of each whack from the glass ashtray. The bartender takes pleasure with each swing that makes the biggest impact. The warm flow of my blood begins to flow down my face and onto the bar into a small puddle. I see it accumulates quickly and I realize that I'm in trouble. I fear when or how this is going to end, continuing to struggle, losing my energy. I crumple face down on the bar into the puddle of blood. The big bouncer shouts a command in Chinese to the bartender and the bludgeoning stops. Suddenly, as if cavalry in an old western movie, American Shore Patrol, Chinese police and Australian Shore Patrol enter with night sticks and calm again comes over the room. The gorilla, sensing that I've had enough, brings me up and presents my bloody mask to the SP's. My face is a mess. Limp and dazed from the pounding I've just endured, the American Shore Patrol looks at the Gorilla and is tempted to exact a little justice. However, once gaining control over my senses, Pardo and I are shown the door.

Outside the bar Pardo and I are greeted by a crowd of curious onlookers. With horrified grimaces, hundreds of Chinese outside the bar snap photos of my bloody mask. They pointed at Pardo's and I ripped clothing. The flash bulbs pop as if Pardo and I are the main attraction in some sort of freak show in a surreal circus. Blue lights flashing, our ride awaits. The paddy wagons of the Hong Kong Police wait patiently as the side doors swing open. A sharply dressed Hong Kong policeman invites us both inside with a swing of his arm and white gloved hand, he points the way inside.

Shore Patrol gets the details from the bouncers' side of things as Pardo's arm is bandaged up and I'm given a cloth to place on my head. As we wait the bouncer that got the best of a bar stool is wheeled out on a stretcher. Gigi comes out of the club and to the paddy wagon. She begins to cry when she sees my face and clothing. "It'll be o.k. Gigi" I comforted her. "I'll catch up with you at the fleet club tomorrow if I can o.k." She nods and continues to cry. Her face grimaces when she looks upon the trails of blood streams that intersect into dark red lines upon my face. The doors to the paddy wagon slam shut and Pardo and I wonder if we'll be taken to a Chinese jail or where?

The paddy wagon pulls away and we take a few turns down the side roads and arrive at the pier where the Proteus is berthed. The Proteus never looked so good. Outside the pier was a little building with a couple of windows and the lights were on. The paddy wagon stops and a polite Hong Kong police opens the door and relinquishes Pardo and me to the shore patrol. We are led to the little building. The doors open to the little building and Pardo and I are led inside. Within, the officer of the watch, an on-duty corpsman and a few Shore Patrol watchmen are waiting. The corpsman grimaces as he sees Pardo and I enter. "What the hell happened?" the officer of the watch asks. The corpsman sits me down in a chair to examine my head. I tell him the events that took place as he writes in his log book and the corpsman cleans the gash in my head from the glass ashtray. As I'm explaining the events, the corpsman stitches up my head and attends to Pardo. "O.k. Torres, let's have that liberty card and your i.d. You're grounded for now until the Supply Officer has a word with you. The club isn't going to press charges on you if you don't press charges on them. I suggest you don't". Pondering my fate, I realize the bouncers have gotten the best of me, that's why no charges. I agree not to press charges and am led by Shore patrol back to the brig onboard the ship for reporting.

The next day I report to the Supply Officer and explain the events of the previous evening. He pauses for a moment, considers the circumstances and fumbling with my i.d. card and liberty card he shuffles them across his desk towards me. "I'm sure she wasn't a dog." gave back my cards. I've never sighed relief as I have up until that moment. Getting back to division I tell my friends and others on the mess decks what had occurred to me the night before. My shipmates listen and I can feel their anger at me being outnumbered. I told them of how Pardo jumped in to help me and paid the price of a broken bottle stabbed into his forearm, and how it was ten against two. My shipmates agree that it was bullshit. That evening twenty of my shipmates and friends arrived at the fleet club to exchange our money. As luck or fate would have it I ran into Gigi and some of her friends. Walking down the hallway she is with her friends. "Gigi!" I yell down the hall. She sees me and runs to me with big smiles, her friends speaking in Chinese and pointing to me as if to know who she was hugging. She nods and acknowledges them and they join us for a drink and a dance. My friends and I agree that we are going back. Back to no other place than Suzy Wong's Pussycat Club. My shipmates will be with me, and this time things will be different.

Upon entering the Pussycat Club, Gigi on my arm, with all of her friends with my friends, pushed through the crowd and took a few tables near the ones the night before. Seeing my shipmates with me and in number, the gorilla and his buddies were quiet and the bartender served us all the drinks we wanted. Gigi and I danced all night and she took me back to her apartment, and yes Gigi sent me to sea a happy sailor.

Finally it was time to say goodbye to Hong Kong. It has been a short and eventful five days, but now time to get back to work servicing the fleet. It was cruising on into the Sea of Japan and on to Yokosuka.

Chapter 10

JAPANESE GIGGLES

Tug boats from Hong Kong harbor pull the Old Pig out from the pier and the Proteus' engines begin to turn the screws to the propellers. It's into the open water of the South China Sea. The Sea of Japan beckons as we steam to Sasebo and Yokosuka, the navy base outside Tokyo. It'll be another ten days or so at sea, enough time to remove the stitches in my head, a little souvenir from our hosts in Hong Kong, a souvenir that I would rather forget.

The ship steams along and the crew again acclimates to the rigors of shipboard life. I was experiencing life at sea as a full-fledged West Pac sailor. This trip has been eventful as general quarters are suddenly ordered. "General Quarters! All hands man your battle stations!" the orders are barked over the intercom. It didn't feel like a drill.

Well past the international boundaries the open bridge observes a Chinese fighter jet and questions its intent. A Chinese Mig fighter has decided to take a closer look at us steaming outside its territorial waters. Apparently one last reminder that China is nearby is buzzing the ship. Nervous commands from the officer of the deck to CIC (Combat Information Center) are cautious. Let's just steam along and maybe this cat will get its sniff and go away. Fortunately, this was the case and the cruise became routine.

It had occurred to me at that moment that we are a forward deployed U.S. Naval warship and that the world is still a dangerous place. That our movements were being watched and our ship's importance to the overall function of the fleet was crucial. The old Pig has a big mission and my respect for the old girl grows.

After several days of routine cruising, drills and navy chow, darkness in the night surrounds the ship as the lights of Japanese fishing vessels appear off the bow. The large cranes and nets hauling in loads of fish under the burning lights of the Japanese trawlers, seagulls squawk.

The Japanese village of Sasebo can be seen in the far distance as the lights of the small base draw nearer. Into the bay and the berth the engines stop and we moor to the berth. It was late and the midnight shift in the ADP shop was still at work, running reports. No one had been to Japan or knew what it would be like. The next morning changing our money for Yen, it was 180 yen to the dollar. O.k. Jonnie and I waiting in the line on the mess decks do the math. 1000 Yen per beer, almost six or seven dollars per beer! Yikes. We realize we'll have to be choosy and cheap in Japan.

Jonnie, Don, Dave, Timbo and I change into civilian clothes, Levi jean jackets, blue jeans, and heavy sweatshirts. It's still cold outside this far north. Careful not to bump my newly removed stitches and scar, Jonnie and I spike up our short locks with lathery hair mousse and bathe in cologne, and head for the Quarterdeck for liberty call. We were anxious to experience our first Japanese port. Little cobblestone streets and quaint little shops define the village of Sasebo. Morning dew settles on flowers and Zen fountains that sparkle in the calm of the morning sun, splash with koi fish. The serenity of Sasebo puts us at ease. Japanese children in their snappy school uniforms walk to school, businessmen hopping into little cars to go to work, Mercedes flatbed trucks driving to the wharf to purchase and deliver the night's catch from the fishing boats, Sasebo awakens to a new day.

We walk and explore for miles, trying to figure out what each curbside store or business was. Of course we couldn't read the language or understand much of what anyone said so we had to observe and try to remember the symbols and letters of the Japanese language for future reference. Much like every other foreign port, it was like being on a different planet, with so many strange and exotic foods, customs and clothing. Even social norms were different as many things that Americans would consider off limits, like eating whale blubber, were accepted. And then there were places that didn't accept us. I mean didn't accept Americans. Bluntly and without reservation we were turned away at some restaurants and Japanese pubs that simply stated they didn't serve Americans there. I couldn't believe the acceptance of this type of bigotry by the Japanese. But it was real.

Our shift was the evening shift three o'clock p.m. to eleven o'clock p.m. we needed to head back to the ship. Our shift consisted of data entry and supply processing. We ran reports on large mainframe computer platforms for the morning meetings of the Captain and other Supply Officers to study and make decisions on, not difficult but tedious. After the shift of course there was time to take a little late night liberty and come back after the bars close and get some shut eye, a perfect set up for a bunch of drunken sailors with money to spend. Of course we earned the old cliché' spend money like a drunken sailor, especially in a country where it was eight bucks a beer we would have to slow down on the clichés'.

Kirin Beer is the national beer of Japan. Good full bodied flavor with a little tang at the end. I always thought it seemed a little grainy, but that's just me. Our shift is over and again it's time to hit the Quarterdeck for liberty. We realize however, that our money would not last long in this port, so prior to leaving the base we purchase a couple of six packs of good ol' Budweiser and stick them into the inner sewn side pockets of our good ol' American Levi jackets. Thank God for Levi Straus. He never thought his jackets would be helping our troops in this fashion. Taking our strategy to the nearest Sasebo watering hole we order a pitcher of Kirin. The little Japanese bar was empty and quiet, not much on the ambience but a place to gather and sip our suds. As the pitcher began to empty, we would open our cans of Bud and while the waitress wasn't looking, pour the beer into the pitcher. The waitress would check on our progress occasionally and with a puzzled look couldn't understand how we could continue to drink without the pitcher becoming empty. Our money saving strategy was working. We took advantage of this little strategy for a while. Finishing our pitcher of beer we looked for our regular type of hangouts. Where were the strip joints? Where are all of the loud and smoky bars, packed full of sailors? We were in agony. Sasebo after all, was not that sort of town. Traditional Japanese family values are the norm here. So after a couple of nights of this we decided to stay onboard and save our money for Tokyo. The charm of Sasebo could only last so long.

With the Proteus' work finished in Sasebo, the Proteus heaves to and cruises up the coast to Yokosuka, an American military and navy depot in Japan just a few miles away from the Japanese capital of Tokyo. Now this might be more like it we thought. The air is crisp and clear and the sky bright, we enter the port in fair weather parade uniforms. Manning the rails in true naval fashion, slowly we moor up to the berth. The port is full of American and Japanese naval vessels and the old Proteus takes her place amongst them. The Japanese crewman working on the decks of their new ships, mockingly grin at the Americans and their old ship, sneering as the ship ties up to the berth. Looking down upon the decks of the new Japanese ships from my spot on the rail I'm offended at their arrogant grinning "Yes, you remember the Proteus in Tokyo Bay on surrender day, don't you" I thought to myself. The reputation of the old lady of the Pacific is well remembered in Japan, and it is at this moment, that her significance in history becomes clear to me. I don't consider her the Rusty Pig anymore and I become proud to serve aboard her.

Finishing our shift that night we take our regularly scheduled liberty. I and the regular complement of buddies take the late subway train into Tokyo. Walking through the subway tunnels the Japanese people bustle. I couldn't understand that it was late at night and businessmen are still going home from work. Secretaries, clerks and other Japanese women are also still working or commuting home. The Japanese people see tall Americans within their midst dressed in blue jean jackets, and mousse spiked hair. Jonnie and I get the smiles from flirty Japanese girls, waving from the windows of the subway cars, while Don and Timbo try to figure out the maps on the wall. Our mission was to find the Tokyo Hard Rock Café'. Finally picking our route we take our train into the dark subway tunnels of Tokyo. Packed into the cars like sardines we are the big ugly Americans amongst the Japanese passengers. The subway train finally squeaks to a stop and emerging from the tunnels into the bustling streets of Tokyo we become small amongst the bright lights and skyscrapers. Bright flickering lights and neon signs line the sidewalks of high rise buildings and skyscrapers. A modern metropolis and there is nothing that I can read or understand. I might as well have been walking on the moon. We walk and take in the exotic culture asking Japanese people, "Hard Rock?" Politely some point in the direction we're walking and we thank them and continue. When out of the confusion and Japanese written neon signs, a beacon of hope, written in English, "Hard Rock Café'! We've made it. After seeing restaurants along the way filled with Foo-goo fish, sushi and whale blubber, a familiar American landmark. Give me a Fuckin Cheeseburger!

We enter the restaurant and there in the air, the familiar smell. A smell that I haven't experienced since I left from San Diego, the smoke from the grill, French fries bubbling up in deep vats of hot grease. I loved it. Old guitars from famous rock and roll icons line the walls. Memorabilia of my teenage idols, autographs and other items tell me that this is the authentic deal.

We found our way to the tables and did the first thing on our regular agenda, order a beer. We settle in and meet other Americans, either living in Tokyo or stationed on the base and begin conversations and enjoy the familiarity of the language. Of course several Japanese people were there as well enjoying the taste of the Hard Rock. We were enjoying our beer and greasy French fries and after drinking large pitchers of that frothy amber nectar of the gods, it was time to be excused to the restroom.

The hallway to the bathrooms was crowded with several young Japanese women. Dressed in the Madonna type fashion striped leggings, molly ragtime style tutus with pink and purple highlighted hair, the Japanese girls nearly choke off the hallway to the head. I find the men's room and enter through saloon style doors. Pushing open the saloon style doors the flap and flip back and forth. I was surprised at the lack of privacy as the urinals can be seen quite easily over and between the openings of the saloon doors. I'm nearly ready to pop. Oh the relief, I thought. My head tilts back, eyes closed, it has been a long subway ride. After a few seconds, "Hee hee hee... hee hee" I raise my head, what the heck? Returning to the matter at hand I hear again..."Hee hee hee". What the heck is that, someone laughing? Raising my head I look around to the saloon doors. To my astonishment, standing there peeking over the doors are several of these Japanese women giggling and watching me pee! I couldn't believe it. What the hell are they doing? O.k. it's their country and I guess it's acceptable to peek at people doing their business and then the thought struck me. "No, Charlie, don't do it" I thought. Being half drunk and of course wanting to score, I decide to fill their eyes a little more. Shaking off the last little bit, "Hee hee hee" they giggle...I give it an extra wiggle and shake. There, I thought, there's an American puppet show for ya. A beef diet has its advantages. Careful not to zip up too quickly, the women continue to giggle and stare.

I wash up and head for the saloon doors and they look at me smiling and giggling. But at that moment as fate would have it, another guy enters the bathroom and they soon forget about me and return to their peep show. The giggling begins again as if they are here for that American experience beyond any others the Hard Rock was offering. I thought I had sold them on my show, but struck out again.

Returning to the tables I share my experience with the guys and the little group of other Americans sitting at our tables.

Talking over beers and into the night I noticed one of the females at the table was really beginning to take interest in me. Before the night was over I was sucking face with the girlfriend of one of the American tourists visiting Tokyo. He watched as his girlfriend tickled my tonsils right in front of him. I don't know if she was trying to tease him or make him mad or what, but I wasn't complaining.

We all decided to change bars and take in a little Tokyo had to offer. The other American's that are joining us give us a word of caution, "You understand that we can only get into a few night spots. We are not welcome at the Japanese clubs". Timbo and Don decided to head back to the ship and reminded Jonnie and I, "The last train leaves at two o'clock a.m. If you miss it, another one won't run until seven." Don said. "See ya later guys" Jonnie said as he and I went off the small group of tourists. Popping into little night clubs we walk the streets of Tokyo after each one. The tourists seem to know they're way around, this little hole in the wall, around this corner or that, they lead on to bar after bar that accepts Yanks in their midst. Eventually after a short while of smooching with the other guy's girl, we stop at an outside elevator that leads to a penthouse night club. The tourist shouts at his girlfriend and me, "You can stop smooching each other now" and grabs her arm. A tug of war ensues between the tourist and me with each arm of the girlfriend. Stop! She said. Shaking her arms from both of our grasps, and makes her choice, chooses her boyfriend as the ruckus is in full swing. At that moment Japanese security for the building arrives and threatens to call the police. Jonnie trying to keep the peace, "It's o.k. we're leaving". I realize I didn't want to spend the next couple of months in a Japanese jail eating fish heads and rice. We leave the tourist and his fickle girlfriend. "Bye" she says as we depart, blowing a sarcastic kiss. What the hell was I thinking? Jonnie and I ponder at what her game is but brush it off as just another unusual experience.

Trying to get into other Japanese night clubs Jonnie and I were rejected entrance simply because they didn't serve Americans there or they were closing. We realized it's getting late, and we forgot about the train. Looking down at my watch surprised it's almost two o'clock. "Jonnie, we forgot the last train is leaving in a few minutes, holy shit!" Jonnie and I bolt for the subway tunnels. Which way, which way was it this way or down there? We couldn't figure out our bearings. We had made too many turns and down strange back alley ways we had lost our bearings. The signs were all in Japanese, we realized we were lost!

Finally after walking many sideways and streets, figuring that we've seen this sign or that one before, we found our way back to the subway tunnels and realized we may be stranded. Inside the tunnels Japanese janitors in blue jumpsuits are emptying trash cans and mopping the floors. "The train?" Jonnie asks one of them. "No train" he replied. "We are totally fucked!" I said. We climb the steps to the outside and think, is the Hard Rock still open, no. Sitting down on a hard concrete bench, "What the fuck are we going to do?" Jonnie ponders. "We'll have to wait for seven o'clock," I said but where. No money for a pricey Tokyo hotel. Hell we only had about fifteen bucks left between us. O.k. money for the train that leaves eight bucks, there was no way. Our little concrete bench was going to be our home for the night. Sitting there like two idiots it's amazing how quiet and deserted Tokyo streets become after two a.m. Shivering with cold our jean jackets barely provide enough warmth when luck has our back again, as in so many other situations. A hot coffee in a can machine is over by one of the buildings. Throughout the long cold and quiet Tokyo night we purchase the hot coffees in a can and press them into our bodies, and as the coffee eventually loses its heat, we consume the beverage to keep the heart pumping. Careful not to spend the train money, and with sore asses from sitting on a concrete bench all night, the hours tick by. Eventually the sign lights flicker back on and the station unlocks the heavy tine gate that leads to the underground tunnels. We have survived our night on the cold bench and head back to the Proteus.

Back at the ship we settle in and remain until we leave the Japanese port back to Guam. The cruise is over and it's time to head back to our homeport and say goodbye to Japan.

Chapter 11

A SEA WITCH NAMED MARGE

After four months at sea, the Proteus returns to Guam. Waiting on the pier, jubilant children yell for their sailor fathers manning the rails at a fair weather parade. We line the rails in our dress uniforms. Lonely wives in flowing dresses waiving with glee, await us on the pier. Bonnie is no exception as Don is waving from his spot on the rails. It's definitely a happy homecoming. Don is scheduled for leave and says goodbye to us and the ship for a few weeks and into Bonnies' open arms. A few days off have been authorized for the crew. The ship's stores are low and I'm sure we could probably use some fuel. The crew begins a normal homeport routine. The shift work in the ADP division is going like clockwork, three shifts a day, and a skeleton crew on weekend duty. The sunny afternoons on Guam give way to the islands' familiar little breezes.

Taking the opportunity to get off the ship for the weekend, Timbo, Dave, Jonnie and I decide to put together a camping trip on the north tip of the island inside the Air Force base beach and picnic grounds. Timbo had an old tent somewhere in his garage and being the resourceful person he is, it was on. Finding the nearest liquor store, we loaded the trucks with Styrofoam ice coolers and stocked them appropriately with the correct beverages. Beer, beer and more beer and oh yes, a couple bottles of Smirnoff vodka. We loaded a couple of brown grocery sacks full of beef jerky, potato chips and canned ravioli and took our party to the beach. We found a nice spot under a couple of coconut trees, gathered old coconut husks and driftwood for a fire and set up the five man tent.

The beer flows as we snorkel the shallow coral reef that extends into the bay. Large purple sea anemones carpet the reef like a giant writhing rug. Little orange and black clown fish dart among the tentacles, as the beer buzz enhances the experience, until dusk we begin to settle next to the fire. Eating our fill of the ravioli and potato chips we share stories of the West Pac cruise. Dave, "Hey let's crack open that vodka!" Taking a nicely chilled bottle of vodka from the Styrofoam chest, he twists open the aluminum cap and crumples it into a little ball. "Hey what if we need that?" Jonnie asks. "We're not going to need it" Dave replies with an ornery grin, as he throws the little balled up cap at Jonnie's chest. Dave takes a cigarette from the box of Marlboro lights in his teeth and clicks open his Zippo lighter. Lighting his smoke, he begins the familiar slug and pass of the bottle around the fire to each of us. We all take slug upon slug until the bottle is empty. The Boy Wonder, Jonnie and I hitting it hard with each pass around the fire until some are passed out on the sand and others crash in the tent. More debaucheries drinking and taking midnight plunges into the dark water of the beach to stay as coherent as possible my last memory of the night…well I can't remember.

The next morning "Get 'em outta here!" I am rudely awakened to Jonnies' New England draw shouting as someone is grabbing my feet. I have found my way into the tent but can't remember how I ended up there. "Oh god you sick bastard!" Jonnie shouts. Taking my feet and dragging me from the tent Dave rolls me out of the tent and onto the sand. Cussing like a sailor, "Son of a bitch! You sick bastard!" Jonnie emerges from the tent covered in my vomit. "You puked in your sleep and we've been rolling around in it all night long!" Jonnie yells. A mush mixture of Italian canned ravioli, potato chips, beer and vodka that I had expelled in my sleep covered the floor of the tent. Remembering his vomit shampoo some months before "I owed you that one asshole!" I reply trying to gain my senses. Rolling back into the shade under the coconut trees, I take comfort in the cool morning sand against my sunburned and vomit covered skin.

Another couple of weeks pass and we enjoy our weekend scuba diving and barbeques at Timbo's place. Craggy underwater rock crevices with hundreds of colorful exotic fish were a hopeless temptation to Timbo. His fish collection at his home aquarium was second to none. Crevices, WWII wrecks, deep water coral reef dives, the selection of dive sights was endless. Discovering the world of scuba diving was a productive activity other than partying. But soon the days of fun in the sun were over and it was back to the ship for work.

After a few weeks, another Monday again arrives and Don returns to the shop. Refreshed and cheesin' with a big grin, Don is happy to be home with his wife Bonnie. It was a long cruise for him. Exchanging our weekend adventures with each other Don asks, "Has anyone seen the weather report?" Not really interested in the weather, I mean really Guam was usually hot or....hot. So no I hadn't seen the weather report. "Yeah, there's a storm coming our way. We may have to get out of here." Don said. "What do you mean the ship?" I said. "Yeah there's a typhoon that's headed our way and the ship will have to leave port to avoid it." After another day it became evident that this storm was becoming a more serious threat than anyone thought. The little island breezes were becoming heavier and the skies were getting a little grayer, then the word came down from the brass. The Proteus has to get out of port and head for open water. We've gotta get out of here. The forklifts on the pier become busy as they load ships stores with last minute provisions. Fuel hoses are pumping fuel and supply personnel stock the galley. The sky is getting greyer.

Not really concerned, the crew waives goodbye again to loved ones' on the pier as if this trip was routine. The looks on their faces were not as happy as they were when we arrived back into port. The tug boats push us out back into Apra Harbor and into the Pacific. Once underway the ship's captain voice comes over the intercom "Yes we're going to try and steer around this thing and avoid it. Hopefully we left early enough to steam far enough north". At least this was the hope. Full flank speed the Proteus sails north, the seas choppy and the rain begins to sprinkle. We sit around the weather decks with wind whipping our shirts. The storm can be seen over the horizon in all her blackness, a monstrous sea witch typhoon named Marge.

The Proteus is giving her all to outrun the storm. The swells begin to grow and the rain pelts our faces, it's becoming ominous outside the weather decks. The leisure sunsets of the Pacific have given way to the blackness of the sea witch. The whistle blows over the intercom the order to secure the weather decks is announced. Ship's captain" Looks like we're in for a bit of a ride so keep the decks secured and all should be fine." It would turn out that this was the understatement of the year.

As time passed it became evident that the ship was in the midst of the storm. Thirty foot waves crashed over the bow pounding the ship's nose deep under the swelling ocean, the joints of the old Proteus groaned under the pressure. Heavy tons and walls of water smash into the sides of the ship, smashing with fury, the sailors tossed about inside from one bulkhead to the other. Savagely the black sea witch takes her anger out on the old lady of the Pacific, as the old Proteus propeller raises from the water in one big swell. The ship shimmies and shakes, nearly shaking her apart. We wait in the division looking to the ceiling with every pop and crack of the bulkhead rivets, the fear was palpable.

The sea is taking a 20 thousand ton ship and tossing her around like a cork, the old Proteus strives on as the black sea which spits lightning, beats her with giant waves and furious wind, keeping her sailors within her protective clutch, the old lady of the Pacific takes a beating. The captain's launch and radio antennas are ripped from the ship's rigging, our communications are down. The captain comes over the 1 m.c. announcing without outside communications, we are alone with the storm. The Proteus continues to take a beating when all at once, the ship goes completely dark, and we have lost power. The Proteus is dead in the water. The intercom crackles, "General Quarters, man your statio...ns!" and crackles quietly.

Taking our orders the sailors of the Proteus know this is not a drill, this is it. Small battery powered battle lanterns flicker on in the dark passageways. The sailors going to and from their stations enter and leave the light like moths entering and leaving the light of porch light the expressions on their faces are grim and serious. They realize we all could meet our watery grave.

For another twelve hours the Proteus is beaten by the black sea witch Typhoon Marge, tossing around the seas without power, without communications and a crew that is confessing their sins to the ships chaplain in the crew's lounge. A fear that I will never forget, my mortality was real in my mind. "Not this way, not like this, my mother won't have anything to bury" I pray my confessions, the confessions of this drunken sailor. The crew fights with the sea and dogs the hatches creating watertight integrity. The old Proteus buckles and shimmies with every punch the sea witch typhoon can dish out. Fighting back the torrent of waves and wind the old lady of the Pacific holds together. Rolling to one side and then to the other the ship is heaving against the heavy waves and rough seas. Up one thirty foot wave and crashing down upon another the Old Proteus fights against the raging typhoon.

The Proteus takes wave after wave of the furious beatings by the wind and sea, popping, cracking and buckling bulkheads groan with pain, the crew's fear will last a lifetime.

The storm subsides and power is slowly restored. The main lights pop and flicker back on, the crew realizes we may have made it out alive from the clutches of Davy Jones' Locker. The black sea-witch had been defeated. The crew can breathe a sigh of relief as the seas relent and the wind calms. The captain and crew take stock of the damage, and realize the old Proteus is one tough seabird built by the greatest generation of world war two.

The crew relieved and battle stations standing down, the sailors of ADP division found all the mainframe computers crashed upon the deck of the processing room. Throughout the ship damage control assessments are being made and shift repairs are taking place. Our antennas and captains launches have been stripped from the decks. Entire catwalks are missing and bulkheads are buckled. We all agree if we had stayed within that storm for very much longer, we wouldn't have made it.

Limping back to Guam battered and bruised, the Proteus pulls into the pier as the families wait patiently. This time there were no smiles, but grimaces and tears as the old Proteus was towed to her berth, ships rigging and catwalks torn from their bulkheads. The families saw the damage first hand and wondered how it was possible to have survived. As the crew disembarks the ship, their fear turns to relief and tearful embraces, as this cruise could have been our last. A battered and beaten ship with a grateful crew, take stock in their victory over the storm. It was that rusty old pig that I saw in the dry dock that got us through. The Proteus had protected her sailors like a mother duck that protects her clutch. She took the violent beating of the sea witch Marge for her crew and I am forever grateful and ask her forgiveness for calling her ugly.

Chapter 12

SAYING GOODBYE

With nearly three years of WestPac cruises under my belt aboard the Proteus, my time onboard was winding down. It was 1988 and my sea duty was coming to an end. I had sailed with the Proteus and her crew to more ports and again experienced more strange things. Discovering something new and unseen with every visit to each port, I finally decided to take in more culture on the last cruise than in previous cruises. I took many pictures with that new camera and experienced more of the culture than night clubs and fist fights. I realized I had a unique opportunity that I probably would never have again. I had grown up. I had now become one of those salty veterans that I originally met at the steel beach picnic, imparting my experiences to the newly arrived sailors with a confident swagger.

Some of the other guys in ADP division get their orders to leave the ship, their sea rotation finished, and are replaced with new faces. Don and Bonnie had gotten orders stateside and left, Dennis from Boston and Jose had left too. Soon it would be my turn. A few more months pass and again we are at sea on a WestPac cruise. Anchored back in Subic Bay the Philippines, it is my turn to leave. My orders have come in and my time aboard the Proteus is over. Timbo decides to throw me a going away party. He and the few buddies that were left from our first cruise together had a sense of loss. We had experienced so much together and now our little group was dwindling down. Only a few of us left from the original cruise. He wanted to make this party special. The little bar he rented out was packed with bikini girls and the entertainment was an act by two Filipino brothers. One who took small darts and blew them from his butt and popped balloons, the other with a painted dartboard on his chest allowing himself to be a human dart board on which the darts from his brothers' ass would have a target. It was an understatement to tell Timbo that I was going to miss his twisted mind.

I said my goodbyes to my division that night, shaking hands we all promised to keep in touch. They were a big part of my life as it was me who was now leaving into anonymousness. I left the little bar with a silken haired beauty and bamboo cup of GORILLA JUICE. Completely wasted, I told Jonnie I'd meet him at the airport the next day as I marched off with a LBFM, for one last hurrah.

Morning arrives and luckily I'm awakened by the twitches of a housefly that had landed upon my forehead. Rising to find I'm in a grass hut, I had no clue where I was. Luckily I find the main street off a muddy backroad and hop into a jeep nee' back to Subic.

Contemplating leaving my buddies that I had known for the last three years I realized they're not just buddies anymore, they had become my brothers. We had been through many adventures together and I pondered my decision to join the military. I concluded that it was a decision that changed my life. My head pounding from the gorilla juice, I check my watch and realize I'm running late. I reached the ship with a few minutes to spare, kudos to the reckless driving of the jeep nee driver.

Freshened up and changed into my tropical whites, I heaved my loaded sea bag upon my shoulder, and took my orders envelope from atop my bare mattress. Pulling the curtain shut one last time and removing the lock from my rack I leave the empty space for the new sailor that soon occupies it. I look around the passageways as I climb the steps to the weather decks and notice life on the ship continues as the crew goes about their daily tasks barely taking notice of my departure. It has become a common place to see sailors coming and going, orders up and leaving for their next duty station, I know the old ship and crew will continue without me. I reach the Quarter deck, "Permission to go ashore sir" I request the officer of the deck. "Granted" is the reply with one last salute. Walking down the steps to the pier I stop, turn and take one last long look at the old Proteus. I must admit I was going to miss her. I say goodbye to the only home I've known for three years, "See ya later old girl, thanks for everything."

After taking a taxi to the airport, I meet Johnny at the airport. He had arrived early. Talking over our experiences and sharing sea stories and lots of laughs while we waited, my flight time had arrived and the announcement to take passengers was made. It was time to say goodbye to the best friend I ever had. I've dreaded this moment, when the eyes well up with tears. I will remember these times. Times I will reflect on with appreciation. With a lump in his throat "We'll keep in touch" he said as he turned, he begins to walk into anonymousness, somewhere in the past, I can't accept him walking into anonymousness, "We'll keep in touch you crazy fucker!" I yell at the last second just before he disappears beyond the gate. He turns with a half smile and wave. I watch him leave.

It was time to board the flight home. I turned to board the plane with the other passengers out to a ladder on the tarmac. There waiting for me was an old stainless steel skinned jet "Flying Tiger Airlines". A Large faded Eskimo face painted in red on the tail section and black fuel stains on the engines. Several rusty rivets surrounded the skin and the paint was slightly peeling. It certainly had seen its' better days as the ladder was wheeled up to the door. It reminded me of seeing the Proteus for the first time, old and clunky, I chuckle away the emptiness of seeing my buddy just leave. Just my luck I thought, leaving the same way I arrived...in "style". I boarded the plane in my tropical white uniform and flew to Alaska. Alaska had three feet of snow on the ground and here I am in tropical white uniform. I had a layover there and appreciated that I was now back on American soil after three years. I was homesick and I had thirty day leave before my next duty station and was scheduled to land in Los Angeles. I planned to visit my father there.

During that flight I looked down through the aircraft window at the landscape of America. After many years in exotic and foreign countries, I missed my country and things familiar. Those things like Thanksgiving parades and pumpkin pie, football games and the crisp air in the fall. I missed summer time days at the beach and the mustard on a Dodger dog at an L.A. Dodger game. I missed Christmas trees and colorful lights on houses. I missed the laughter of my dad and the hugs of my mom. I missed America.

Landing at LAX the plane couldn't land fast enough for me. I couldn't wait to get to my father's house and just relax. I shared my adventures and stories with my family and enjoyed the break. But as my days of leave dwindled, I would have boarded another plane and on to my next duty station with a stop in a little town in lower Alabama to see my mom. I had one last thing I wanted to do before leaving Los Angeles. I needed to see the view from Griffith.

Having said my goodbyes to my Dad, I put on my WestPac Jacket and get into the taxi waiting outside the front door. I went back up to Griffith Observatory that night on the way to the airport. The taxi drives up the winding road on the little hillside we arrive at the concession building and parking lot. The taxi driver nods as I begin to exit, "Keep it rolling, I won't be long" as I get out of the taxi. Getting out across the parking lot I hear the beginning riffs of Stairway to Heaven, a Led Zeppelin song gently playing on an open car door speaker. A small crowd of long haired teenagers congregated around the car waiting for a visit to the Observatory. They laugh and enjoy the carefree moments of their youth. I wondered and amused that just a few years earlier it was me with the long hair and t-shirt. Rocking to riffs on the radio. I realized how I had changed. How this experience has changed me. I had become a sailor. I see myself in their innocence as I turn to take in the view. The skyline twinkles in the dark distance and the Hollywood sign on the hill I begin to reflect. I wondered about my friends back on the old Proteus. Ironically in this town, Hollywood, the land of make believe, what stories and memories I had in those exotic ports and how far away and real they all are. Some countries are still situated in war zones fearing that war will come again, others who people struggle to survive their economic circumstances, political instability and bigotry. I realized that I'm really home and I am thankful to live in this wonderful country. I realized the poverty of my youth did not scare me against the opportunity that I have being American and what I sacrificed to defend it.

I had finally answered the question to myself in boot camp, "was this all going to be worth it? What is the American Dream?" I realized it at this moment. I had been to the greatest adventure of my life. It was worth those long weeks in San Diego boot camp being away from the people I loved, and my broken heart from a girlfriend left behind. It was worth those long hard days in the fire watch department. It was worth the cold night watches in the South China Sea and the anger of Typhoon Marge. It was worth the bad leftovers at midnight meal and the fist fights that preserved my American pride in Hong Kong. I realized the American Dream isn't just about gobs of money. That my idea of success was not what I thought at all. You see the American dream is the preservation of our culture and our rights. The ability to choose your government and not be dictated by it. The freedom to pursue life, liberty and happiness, without repression from a government that has forgotten its role as a public servant. It is the little things that make life worth living. And after it all, seeing other people in foreign countries ravaged by war, attacked by repressive enemies that would take their rights, living in poverty without a responsible government. Other countries that would deny you a glass of water simply because they don't serve Americans, and some taking for granted their American citizenship, I realized that I was the wealthiest man in the world. That I live in a country where I can freely express my speech, my thoughts and pursue my dreams. That a free system of government, if we remain diligent, is for the people and by the people and it shall endure. I had realized the American Dream and knew it was worth it all.

The years passed and I finished my obligation to the Navy. I received my honorable discharge and began my life as a civilian. For this reason or that, I lost touch with all those guys back on the Pig. This was the age before the internet, the late eighties and early nineties. But as several years pass life changes, and occasionally my thoughts revert back to those days on the Proteus. The thoughts of those crazy times when we were young, hitting all those exotic ports. The memories would bring reminiscent smiles to my face.

I eventually married and had kids and a career in Real estate and yes, I put myself through college and got my degree in business administration, until one day my brother, who had recently retired from the Navy, recommended a website www.togetherweserved.com.

I thought well it's been a long time since I've been in but I was open to give it a try. I built my page and profile and as fate would have it within two hours my cell phone rings. It was a phone number I didn't recognize and I answered. "Hello?" I say, "We'll keep in touch you crazy fucker!" mocking my last words at the airport, the voice was unmistakable, a New England draw. After 20 years I had heard Johnnie's voice again.

As I get reacquainted with my buddies from the Proteus, we share our memories of our exploits overseas. Laughter from the good old days from guys that are now in our 40's and a few nearing 50 years old, take us back to our youth. We can't believe it's been so long ago and we are all living our individual version of the American Dream. Those days of the memories detailed here in this book.

Jonnie stayed in the navy and made it a career and is now retired. He is now married and has kids and lives in San Diego working with computers. He's still the same ornery cuss I met 25 years ago.

Don and Bonnie are still married and living in San Diego as well. Both stayed in the navy and retired. Their marriage that stood the test of time, and military separation has proven enduring. They see Jonnie often.

Timbo got out of the navy after his initial tour and is living in Louisiana. He has put his resourcefulness to good use and has become quite the craftsman making expensive furniture from exotic wood.

The "Boy Wonder" is still in the navy and has become a Lieutenant Commander. Go figure.

Totally by luck, I ran into Tiffalo once in Virginia. He is a Sheriff's deputy.

I have not reconnected with Dave from Wisconsin or Dennis from Boston but hopefully, one day will share a few laughs with them again.

After doing some research, I discovered the Rusty Pig, the USS Proteus, was decommissioned and sent to Texas to be cut apart for scrap. As of 2008 the last steel bulkhead was cut and the old Proteus took her place in history. The old lady of the Pacific is gone.

The events in this book are an account of my memories as a young sailor serving overseas. I have taken steps to keep my friends' anonymity intact as some of the names have been changed, but the content is all accurate. The time I spent in the Navy was unique and was made unique by the friends that I shared it with. I will cherish these memories forever. So, until the next port I will say goodbye in true seafarer fashion, I wish you all Fair Winds and Following Seas.

THE END

Printed in the United States
By Bookmasters